CW00345175

To
christie

So fabulous to
meet you & swap
books.

love
Alise x

Alise x

A PATH TRAVELLED

How to Make Sense of Your Life

By Alison Blackler

Copyright @ 2020 Alison Blackler

www.2-minds.co.uk

Alison Blackler asserts the moral right to be identified as the author of this book, in accordance with the Copyright, Designs and Patents Act 1988.

All rights reserved. No part of this book may be reproduced, stored in a retrieval system, or transmitted in any form, or by any means, electronic, mechanical, photocopying, recording or otherwise, without the prior written permission of the publisher.

First published in 2020 by 2minds publishing

Copyeditor and proof readers: Sian-Elin Flint-Freel

Front cover design: Ross Makepeace rossmakepeace@googlemail.com

Typesetting and chapter illustrations: Annie Lawrenson

Photograph: Dan Dawson

Printed and bound: Ingram Spark

ISBN 978-1-5272-5336-0

A Path Travelled - how to make sense of your life

DEDICATION

For Sam, Beth and Eve,

My nephew and nieces — may you always
believe in yourself whatever life brings you and
know that I believe in you all.

" A wonderful reminder that no-one can 'make us feel' anything. So often in life it is not other people's actions that harm us, but how we react to them. This book enlightens readers that by choosing how we feel, react and respond we can choose a new path and a new future. **"**

Jane Loughran
Communications Specialist and former BBC Journalist

❝This book is like going for a lovely walk
with a clever insightful friend, enjoyable,
conversational with just the right amount
of challenge. As you go along your
thinking changes, your mind begins to
clear, and you find you have more choices
and clearer thinking on your return.**❞**

Caitlin Walker

Author of Contempt to Curiosity, creating the
conditions for groups to collaborate and So you
want to be....#DramaFree

"A Path Travelled takes us on a journey of self-discovery, inspiring us to become open to new possibilities and make positive changes in our lives."

Tamsin Hartley
Author of The Listening Space: A New Path to Personal Discovery, and Captured Moments: Poems Inspired by a Listening Space

My Journey...

I started writing this book on a gorgeous, sunny autumnal day in November 2011, down on the beach at Thurstaston, on the Wirral, with my two Labradors playing, chasing and greeting everyone that came along the beach. The only tools I had were banana cake, my iPod and a stunning view for inspiration.

Despite sometimes being a distraction, I knew this view would also unleash the creativity and inspiration within, giving me the time and space to be and the confidence that I could do it. I then continued to write in various locations on and off over 8 years: at home, in cafes, at friend's and often when out walking, capturing it into a voice recorder. It has taken me quite some time! The trick of balancing my work and home life, along with the huge learning curve of writing a book made it quite a task!

For me, I was working for some years in NHS administration, although I always knew, deep down, that working with people was my passion. Until I realised this, my fulfillment was limited and I needed a boost of self confidence to make something happen.

So, I decided to make a change. I continued to work in the NHS, but in much more people-focused roles, working first in health promotion before qualifying as a Counsellor. I progressed to the interesting field of drug and alcohol addiction and domestic abuse. It was during this phase of my career that I started to recognise the potential for enabling people to change their lives for the better. I noticed that there is always something good that comes out of every situation — that we can learn from adversity and develop resilience. I became fascinated about human behaviour and started to notice that people had tools within them so that limits could be explored and problems could be solved.

My work as a Counsellor developed my interest with how people react, why they behave in certain ways and what is behind their response. I became more aware of the roles and games we play in families, what we learn and mirror from our parents, guardians and teachers in the early years and how this then affects future relationships, choices and, ultimately, where we get to in life. This led to qualifying in Neuro Linguistic Programming (NLP) and then on to me becoming a Coach. While developing these skills, I was continually working on myself and my own barriers. This approach allowed me to uncover and understand why things happened to me and what I needed to do to change it.

Over 25 years ago I found myself noticing that I had to take personal responsibility for my own life and yet I did not know how. I became aware that I was going through life, looking outside for the answers and yet missing the answers that were inside me. All the situations and people that have been in my life have been there for a reason, and you will learn that this will be the same for you.

I have often been able to brush myself down after a challenge and move to the next life chapter; although moving on is a good approach, it didn't always quite feel complete as a solution. It was like I was always searching for answers. Despite it being a powerful process to let go of the negative beliefs, reframe memories and reduce negative emotions, what I know now is that I was often missing the vital personal lessons in each situation. Each lesson can help you truly grow and free yourself of your old, unhelpful thoughts and behaviours.

This was a gradual learning curve for me which took many years. The wealth of my journey started to unfold when I realised that I couldn't free myself from my baggage without understanding its purpose and reason and thereby change my thinking. When I say, as I do above, that all things, even the difficult and challenging times or people in your life, are there for a reason, I hope to enlighten and inspire you, so that you realise that everything does happen for a reason - and that reason is personal growth.

There have been big gaps in time while writing this book when I was often working on things myself.

Writing a book like this needed the appropriate time and head space to make it right and authentic. I couldn't write if my thoughts were not sorted in my own mind. This prolonged period gave me the experience and joy of working with many more wonderful people who have shown determination and vulnerability to be able to take the steps to change their lives. Life is certainly a journey and writing this book has been quite a trip!

From the outset and despite all the hard work I put into my manuscript, I never thought it would become a real book. The one powerful thought I need you, the reader, to remember is 'never say never'. Anything is possible, if you believe in it, put your mind to it and be serious about taking action. Buying my book means you have set off on your own path of discovery and taken a step towards a future that is right for you.

Warm wishes

So let's begin our journey together........

A Path Travelled - how to make sense of your life

Chapter Three - What SHAPES Us?   71

Chapter Four -
Experiences & Expectations

Let's Start

Let me tell you what is behind this book and what it is all about. It is a combination of a lifetime of knowledge gained from working with clients, the books I have read, the training and courses I have attended, the people I have met - who have taught me so much – and of course, my own valuable personal life experiences. I feel compelled to share my experiences, my knowledge and my acquired understanding. I believe that sharing my learning with you will help you free yourself from your shackles, to realise your full potential and allow you to start to have the life you want and deserve.

How to use this book

You can use this book as suits you. You can read it through and then come back to the exercises or take your time to work through each section. It has key areas that many of us struggle with and ideas and tools to remedy these issues. I also share the results that we can start to expect and techniques on how to make changes for yourself.

Throughout the book there are exercises to help you reflect on your thinking, behaviours and beliefs, and case studies to demonstrate that you are not alone. Use the book as time and space for you to reflect. Use the simple exercises to guide you. Or if you prefer, just take plenty of time to allow your learning to settle. You may be challenging some deep-rooted beliefs and patterns so baby steps are vital.

You are powerful

The goal is to realise how powerful you are and that you do construct your own life and reality. Once you notice how you do this, you will be able to create your life just as you want it. Together we will unpick and look at things differently. I will show you how to shine and be the best version of you for you. We will explore the idea that there are no actual limits, only ones we place on ourselves. Making changes takes courage, motivation and pure grit but it is well worth the effort once on the other side.

Modern days

Modern days are exciting and full of opportunities and choices but at the same time are full of pressure. If you go back to the Industrial Revolution, people appeared to be simply settled by having a job, a marriage or a friendship and they stuck at it. In modern life there are so many changes and challenges. We, as humans, expect more and it is almost like we are seeing a 'revolution of the mind'. We are much more aware that we can get more from ourselves, but can we really keep up with the speed of society and growth?

In today's world and the fast pace, we feel immense pressure to keep up and constantly do better. We experience relationship and communication breakdowns. Our jobs change. We end up wanting more but are often unsure how to achieve it. Now is the time to learn how to use your mind effectively, to be free from the 'baggage' acquired in life and find an easier way. In this book, together we will look at how our minds function and why we find ourselves thinking, feeling and behaving in certain ways. I believe that if we understand some of the neuro-science behind our actions, then it becomes far easier to make the changes we so badly want.

In pursuit of happiness

We are all on a permanent search for happiness but can often miss that very happiness in the pursuit. We are so often waiting for happiness to come, that waiting becomes the activity, and even a time waster. As Buddha said: "Happiness is the journey not the destination." Now it is time to become proactive in your search...and to enjoy the ride.

Your perfect outcome may be to find your soul mate, to have a great job or generally a life ideal for you. While the perfect partner, job, or life may be out there, you must first feel settled and happy within yourself. You need to know more about the real you. To do so, you will need to free yourself from unhelpful thinking and behaviours, which can be linked to family traits and past experiences. A shift in your thinking and beginning to understand the helpful lessons in challenging situations, is a gift to move you forward.

A shared sense

This book is full of theories, ideas and tips to help you along the wonderful journey that is life, but before we go any further I am keen for you to get a sense of belonging.

It is very powerful for you to know that there is always someone else that is feeling the same as you or experiencing a similar situation to you. When you are able to talk about your feelings, there is a sense of relief that you are not alone. Loneliness with difficult memories, negative beliefs, thoughts and emotions is a challenging place. Know that I am writing this having been on my own journey. Many of my experiences will have been the same as yours. While everyone around me would say that I always bounced back during challenging times, inside it was often a very different story. I can put on a 'brave face' although this can be exhausting and draining. So, know that you are not alone, not on an island with your confusion, pain or sadness.

Wherever you are or whatever you would like to change right now is where we will start. Together, we will take a look at your challenges from a different perspective. When I learnt to understand why things happen, to look differently, I took action and made steps towards an alternative solution and better future. This is what I want for you.

Changing direction

Sometimes we find ourselves on a path which doesn't quite feel right. We can be there because someone else thinks it is the right direction or perhaps we have actually outgrown the situation or person. I have experience of this and yet until I realised my fulfilment was limited, I needed a boost of self-confidence to make something happen, so I took action and made changes.

We can go through life and not fully understand why we react in the way we do. We seem to accept that 'this is the way it is' and don't realise that we can change more than we know. We quite often put up with difficulties and scenarios without question — C'est la vie!

In this book, we will explore what influences us to go down some paths in life. Are we meant to go down some of those difficult paths to learn something great about ourselves? Probably. Or is it a message that we need be clearer about our own wants and dreams, to be assertive with others and to truly connect with ourselves. Others can be a great influencer although it doesn't always make them right.

The valley of blame

We will be exploring many of the behaviours that keep us stuck in situations, relationships, jobs and life in general. One very common scenario is getting stuck in what we can call the 'valley of blame'. We end up blaming ourselves or others rather than looking closely at each situation. We often blame everyone else for making what feels like the same mistakes again and again. However, by doing this we may be missing the reasons why things and people were 'sent' into our life. For me, I now know that all the situations and people that have been in my life have been there for a reason, a good one, even though it may not have felt it at the time. Taking personal responsibility for our own lives takes courage and energy. We often know that we need to, although don't know how. We often look to the outside for the answers, overlooking the fact that many of the solutions are inside.

Moving on from difficult times can be complex and painful. Sometimes we are searching for the answers yet looking in the wrong places. This book will guide you to moving on in a powerful and different way, allowing you to understand limiting beliefs, reframe memories and manage negative emotions, all using your powerful mind. The trick is not to miss the vital, often hidden, personal lessons which are continually being presented. We usually miss these because we are busy blaming someone else or focused on the details of the situation. Each lesson can help you truly grow and free yourself of your old, unhelpful thoughts and behaviours.

The good news

I have distilled what I have learned and written it in this book. I want to share this with you so your understanding and your 'light bulb moments' come quicker for you than they did for me. Within this book, we will develop that much needed instruction manual for your thinking and behaviours. We will look at the influence's others have had on our lives and learn that we are most fulfilled when we are on our own path.

We will take time to look at our unhelpful thoughts, feelings and behaviours. Why we do them, how habits are formed and the part limiting beliefs play in holding us back. We all struggle with the complexity of our minds, so I hope this book will be of great use.

The tools

When I am working with people, I talk about a toolkit which is full of different tools and approaches for different scenarios. Throughout the book I will be sharing some of those tools. You will learn the importance of being aware. You will identify steps you can take to challenge your thinking. How to let go of negative habits and learn to change your thinking and behaviours so that you can find a new, positive, different path. We will be looking for a different view of the world, to start to guide your thinking and produce an alternative result. The impact of your inner world is something that you experience in everyday life. Being aware of what that is, is a vital part of the journey. I believe that if we understand the why, then we are more likely to work out the 'how' and make significant changes.

CHAPTER TWO

The POWER is YOU

We will begin this journey by looking at some of the functions of the mind, how things are processed, how we interpret what is around us and then what happens as a result. Don't panic, this is only a tiny bit of theory to look at how the clever mind works! As you read through this chapter, ideas are introduced which will be explored in more detail later in the book. You may have questions and start to wonder how you address your own issues. Keep reading as the answers will come. As you and your mind travel together you will learn to train it to work even more efficiently.

So just to get you off on a very strong foot – keep in mind you are way more powerful than you can imagine. The human mind is so powerful and is there to support, protect and run your life, as well as your body. It is your very own number one fan and your constant companion at every step of your life.

It is the power of your mind that determines *every* aspect of your reality and it is your individual choices that determine what you will or will not experience. Your mind has unlimited potential. Just consider, for a moment, how amazing you are? You may be able to connect with some of your potential greatness although there is always more!

As Nelson Mandela said "Our deepest fear is not that we are inadequate. Our deepest fear is that we are powerful beyond measure". Believe it or not you can create almost anything you desire in your life, by training the mind to achieve it. The mind is wired to create connections with past experiences and to learn habits. It can be considered the engine of your body. The brain is like a futuristic super motorway where the traffic moves in many directions and never stops. The exciting thing is that it is possible to develop the ability to use this power even more. Have you ever truly looked at how many things your mind has lead you to achieve in your life so far? Take a few moments to think about this, as you are likely to have missed them and are focused on what you haven't achieved.

When you begin to understand the strength of the mind, you can adjust the focus of your attention and start to lead a fulfilled life. When you use this powerful tool effectively and positively, you will start to notice that there are always options and often different, easier ways to tackle any problem.

Sound great? Read on.

The brain and mind

Firstly, a little bit of real science for those who are interested. Do you know the difference between your brain and mind? The brain is physical; it weighs about 3lbs and sits neatly in your skull. The mind is your awareness, thoughts, feelings, sensations, internal images and where your dreams and desires are created.

We have 100 billion active brain cells and there is a myth that we only use approximately 1 - 1½ % in our lifetime. This has been proven to be untrue; in fact, we use many more brain cells and yet there are still much more we could use.

The unconscious mind is processing roughly 11 million bits of information every second, although we are not aware of much of it. Most of this information is carefully managed by our mind, almost on 'our behalf'! Despite us being in the possession of this powerful machine, we rarely maximise its strength and possibility, especially in a positive way.

Your mind at work

Let's explore the mind, your power centre. The mind is about perception, thinking, judgement and memory. This is how you are aware of the external world and your experiences, how you think and feel, your sense of consciousness and your emotions. It is where reasoning and thoughts happen, and it is extremely influential and impressive. You have access to something more powerful than the most sophisticated computer system and yet so commonly don't know how to use it. Without knowledge and training, it is like having no instruction manual!

Many of you may already know there are two distinct parts to the mind: the conscious and the subconscious.

Understanding more about how each part works can help you to make sense of what is happening within you. Then you can learn how to get the most out of this powerful asset.

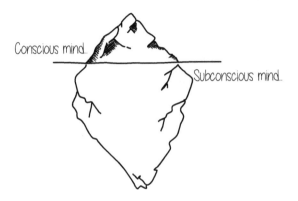

A great way of describing these parts of the mind is to think of a giant iceberg. What we see on the surface of the water is tiny compared to what lies beneath. The visible tip represents the conscious part. The subconscious is equivalent to the much larger invisible part of the iceberg and is extremely powerful. The conscious mind likes to think it is in control, though anyone who has ever studied the workings of the mind knows differently.

The conscious mind

The conscious mind is the rational part. It can set goals, make decisions, think logically and create reason. It aims to make sense of everything, although this happens more effectively when we take a little time to stop and think. This part represents no more than 12% of the total mind's capacity. When we decide to make a movement, such as raising a hand or leg, it is done by the conscious mind.

So, whenever you are aware of what you are doing, you can be confident that you are using your conscious mind. If there is a cup of coffee beside you and you decide to take a sip, this process will be done by your conscious mind. You made the decision to drink and you were aware of what you were doing. The subconscious minds' activities can be less in our awareness and therefore unconscious.

The subconscious mind

What is the subconscious mind? It can also be called the unconscious mind. To avoid confusion, I will use the term subconscious mind throughout this book.

The subconscious mind's main functions are all the involuntary and automatic actions; it is working 'behind the scenes' for us. Our breathing, heartbeat and all the physical functions of the body are controlled by our subconscious mind. We do not have to remember to breathe or blink! It also stores our emotions, beliefs and memories.

The information it holds is a blend of everything we see, hear, feel, taste and smell. It is where all habits and behaviours are created. All the habits, whether they are in our thinking, actions or what we have learned, create a groove in our minds.

Imagine each habit or pattern creates a mark in the network of your mind. It can be called a neural network – like telephone exchange boxes dotted about at the corner of roads. But we are all different and all have a different set of grooves in our networks. We have a groove for absolutely everything we do, which means they will be repeated; from how you put your shoes and socks on, to what you think about yourself and how you respond to anything else. We have created a habit for pretty much everything, good and bad, often without even realising.

One of the miraculous functions of the subconscious mind is that it processes automatically and constantly. The conscious mind on the other hand, tends to be able to focus on one thing at a time and could not possibly cope with the amount of information being processed subconsciously. It would become overloaded, so the subconscious manages the millions of pieces of information coming at us constantly and continually.

Imagine the subconscious mind being like a huge store room of all our experiences in life. The subconscious delivers feedback to our conscious mind and these are interpreted as our thoughts. These thoughts direct our emotions and affect our behaviour. The subconscious takes those thoughts, processes them and then an internal reaction is created. This happens constantly and all in an instant.

Our subconscious mind expertly stores an interpretation of absolutely everything with the purpose of keeping us safe. It likes to keep everything 'just in case'. We wouldn't be able to remember everything if we had to consciously process. Just know that it is all stored somewhere, and that is why randomly we can recall a situation from years ago. We see, hear or feel something that triggers off a memory which creates thoughts, feelings and emotions automatically based on what is already stored. It can be good or bad experiences; both act as a safety net to survive and the mind will alert us whether it believes something or someone is safe or not.

So how do we make sense of it all?

Through our experiences, the information stored is constantly being updated and alters the version of ourselves and our reality. This map of our reality becomes our own truth. It is from here that we create beliefs, habits and behaviours. It never stops updating. We each create an interpretation which is like an internal imprint of the reality, a picture in our mind of what we 'think' has just happened. We are often unaware that our view of the world has been largely created based on information which has been previously processed and stored internally.

Let's just look at a little more theory as it is important to help you understand it's working. More manual pages!

A clever feature built into our minds is a function that will filter a large portion of the mass of information, so that we can make sense of the world. This stops us becoming frazzled, over wrought by the millions of pieces of information and messages we receive. The skill of our subconscious mind is to try and distinguish between what is relevant and what needs to be ignored. If we tried to make these distinctions consciously, we would not be able to do anything else. We would be exhausted. It would be impossible to decipher and process every single detail from each moment.

The subconscious mind has specific filters to separate what it perceives to be important for each of us. Otherwise, it would be like our 'store room' being completely disorganised and chaotic with all the information just dumped in there. These filters sift through the information and help us to make sense of it all. What we mean by information is things we see, hear, feel, taste and smell. Our 5 senses.

We all interpret situations uniquely. For example, two friends attending a music festival together will both have a slightly different experience based on their internal processing. One may be relaxed and happy, while the other has a memory of being lost at a previous festival and is anxious all the time.

One of the key things that make us all different is our own belief system. This affects our 'map of our reality' and is what we use to navigate through life. The mind makes decisions based on what is stored within. For example, you are thinking about your health and well-being and you want to get fit. Your map of your reality could say that you need to be in great shape before you join the gym. You may have decided that everyone else in the gym will be super fit, toned and you will feel intimidated. You then make a decision (almost instantaneously) that it is not the right time to join the gym and nothing changes.

This example highlights that whatever you think you are or think about is just a fraction of the truth. It is not true that you need to be super fit to join a gym, yet you have made it a truth. Whatever is stored in your subconscious mind will in some way affect hopes and usually hold you back. Paying attention to this is vital.

Self-sabotage

When we have conflict with ourselves, it is often a challenge between our conscious desire and our subconscious mind trying to protect us. This can manifest as something we will call self-sabotage, a true battle of the minds! We all seem to self-sabotage at times, some more than others. This is where we get in the way of ourselves and limit our potential. If the subconscious mind doesn't think it is possible, it will do everything and anything to stop you! Remember its job is to protect you.

All experiences create a memory within and from here we can construct a set of beliefs about ourselves. As with anything in life, some of these are clearly good and help us, while others are negative and limiting. There are many people who have created a belief that they are not good enough. As humans we compare ourselves to others, limit our achievements and generally create doubts about ourselves. We often have a tendency to interpret situations against ourselves and then 'make up' that people don't like us, or we have upset them. For example, when someone appears to ignore you, doesn't reply to a message or is whispering with a friend, you can automatically interpret this to mean that you have done something wrong.

While this clearly could be true, it is more often the case that we have mixed our own feelings in with what we think we are experiencing. We so often misinterpret other's actions. This processing all happens in a blink of an eye and you are left with an emotional response related to the thoughts. You feel upset, angry or even devastated. By starting to understand this whole cycle, we can see issues differently and get an idea of what holds us back.

Our 'auto pilot'/fight, flight or freeze response

Before we look more deeply at what limits us, let's just quickly have a look at another natural and yet often misinterpreted function of the mind. We have an auto response to danger, often called 'the fight, flight or freeze' response. Most people understand the basics of this response, but it is worth understanding how it works and how it can confuse the situation.

It is important to remember that fight, flight and freeze is natural and occurs when the mind senses imminent danger; something is perceived as a threat and immediate action is needed, just like it would if we were in the jungle. This is the oldest part of the human mind and we need it to keep us safe. Adrenaline is quickly pumped through the body which elevates the heart and respiration rate.

This delivers maximum energy to all the cells in our bodies, giving us a burst of superhuman strength. There are lots of examples of people lifting cars off people who are trapped, running into burning buildings to save others, and outrunning attackers who would do them harm. This is a perfectly normal response and necessary to our survival.

The loyalty of our mind and the speed at which it reacts to protect and alert us to a situation is faultless. It is instantaneous. However, our subconscious mind does not know the difference between something that is a real danger and a creation in the mind. For example, if we watch a scary movie, our pulse rate increases even though there is no actual danger. As it can't differentiate, the subconscious will assume that there is a real threat rather than an imagined one.

Perceived danger

With this understanding, know that the mind can also spring into a fight, flight or freeze response in situations which are not actually a physical threat and yet it has interpreted them to be. Our bodies are put into red alert instantly when the mind has interpreted a situation as fear based.

Logical thinking, at that moment, often isn't available; we react and, more often than not, overreact. An example could be that someone is concerned that the boss is not happy with their work and an email pops into their in-box with the subject '1:1 meeting'. This sends the person into an instant panic as they interpret this to mean that they are in trouble. The mind has created a response, maybe an anxious feeling, which it then perceives as dangerous, yet the employee has just probably 'made up' the outcome based on their own fear.

Whilst this is a natural response, there is ultimately a choice as to what happens next. We can push ourselves to overcome the feeling, both physically and mentally, such as in a presentation, an interview, a date, a marathon or a speech at a wedding. Trying something new and uncertain is naturally going to trigger heightened responses.

The mind doesn't like it when we don't know what to expect and it must work really hard to manage this. It is a fine art to notice which came first, the feeling or the thought. It is this that makes it feel like there is no control. For example, you are going to give a presentation, maybe the thought is a fear of something bad happening, of showing yourself up, a fear of failure or embarrassment. Or do you first notice the physical symptoms, like churning in your stomach and this becomes your focus. While you stay focused on these physical feelings, such as the increased heart rate, hot hands, shaky legs or butterflies in the stomach, these then tend to amplify and you can feel like you are out of control. This response does nothing to help the situation, as these symptoms are in auto-pilot now. It is from this position that we adopt the fight, flight or freeze response, which means we often make unhelpful choices and decisions in that moment.

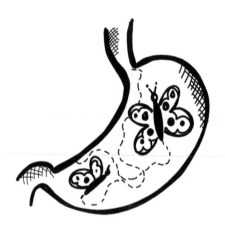

Whilst we are saying that this is a natural response to keep us safe, at times it can be unhelpful and even confusing. For example, the symptoms of excitement and anxiety can be very similar. You might feel them both in your stomach or heart area. Have you noticed that your heart beats faster when you are excited and similarly as much as when you are nervous? What is important is to be aware of these responses, to understand their purpose. Then you can start to control your physical response by settling the mind. This will then alter your behaviour. It really is all in the mind! Later we will look at how the mind interprets fear linked to limiting beliefs we have about ourselves and how this plays out.

Interpreting the world

For now, though, we will just reinforce the function of the mind. Everything that has happened, every minute, every second, every event is all stored in the subconscious. This includes everything from your childhood memories, beliefs you hold about yourself, decisions you have made, your values and attitudes, experiences at school, stories with relationships, friendships, how your parents communicated with you, and your work life. Your mind keeps all this information for reference in the 'store room' and it is this information that is used to interpret or measure current events.

With all this in mind, we understand that we see the world not as it is, but how we perceive it to be. In fact, as we believe it to be. We see, feel and understand the world through our own personal lens, which means that our view will be very different from everyone else, making each of us unique. Just like we all have our own fingerprints, we also have our own way of processing and understanding the world. We are all able to distort or muddle up what has been said or done, which has a huge and varied effect on our responses. It is this uniqueness that causes many of the communication problems between each of us. It is virtually impossible to actually understand something from another's perspective, but knowing that allows us to be more flexible and accommodating.

In summary, our minds are processing millions of pieces of information continually. Thankfully there are a set of filters which help with this processing, so let's understand how these work.

Personal in-box

Let's now look at what happens to all this information that we are processing, coming through our 5 senses. Imagine that the information coming in are like emails into your in-box. The filters need to work out what is important, what needs action, what can be safely ignored and what can go straight in the junk. We have filters in the subconscious mind to help to manage and process the information and ultimately to keep us safe. By looking at these filters, we can make sense of how we all personally represent the world.

Delete or ignore button

It is true that the subconscious mind holds onto and manages all information which doesn't come necessarily into our conscious awareness. A simple example is the subconscious mind manages information around our body temperature and will only bring this into our awareness if there is an action required, like putting on or removing a jumper. Because there is so much information coming in at any one time through our 5 senses, it will delete external stimulus when no action is required. Without a delete function the mind would blow a metaphorical fuse.

Another example of this is noticing how many situations there are when there is a background noise which stays in the background. We are familiar with what it is, so the mind blocks it out as not important. This is obvious when you know the common sounds in your house which you ignore and you only become aware when it is unusual. The mind can even do this for the alarm clock when you really are not wanting to get up!

Another healthy example of this filter working well would be when another person's name is being called out in a waiting room. The subconscious mind doesn't pay much attention to this name as it is not relevant to you, so what is being said is by passed – until, of course, your name is called. We selectively pay attention to certain aspects of our experience.

This filter is really useful for so many situations although it does also have a negative side. There are some situations, linked to how you feel about yourself, when information can be deleted inappropriately. This internal response can change your perception dramatically and can result in the situation being misinterpreted. An unhealthy example of the deletion button is when we might ignore positive feedback which does not fit with our internal thinking. It may be a negative belief or image we hold about ourselves being activated. Someone says, 'You look lovely today' and instantly you dismiss this comment because you are not feeling good about yourself. We might notice a negative internal feeling or a thought like, 'they can't mean it'. These responses are a result of limiting beliefs, which ultimately constrain us.

Distortion button

Another interesting feature of our filters is their ability to distort. Our minds can appear to twist a situation and misrepresent the reality. This then affects our response. There are many ways of distorting information, such as making assumptions, being self-conscious, paranoid or blaming others. All these are generally linked to what we believe about ourselves and the experiences we have in our memory, rather than what is actually happening.

One basic visual example is when a person who is afraid of snakes may mistake a rope lying on the ground for a snake. A distortion of a situation could be when in a relationship, you could interpret a lack of contact as a sign the other person isn't interested or you may even make up that the relationship must be falling apart. Rational thinking gets overruled in so many situations when we are highly emotional. Often our conscious and subconscious minds are in direct conflict with each other and yet the subconscious mind is so powerful it seems believable.

Another example of distortion is when a manager says to an employee, 'When we have finished the team meeting, can I have a word?' Just like the previous example with the email request for a 1:1, this message can become warped to create an overreaction. The team meeting is then an agonising process for this employee. He or she may have created a scenario that they are in trouble or even an extreme that they are going to lose their job. They are unable to concentrate and don't perform at their best, having already decided the outcome in their head. Hang on though, let's just rewind that scenario. Maybe the manager wanted to praise them or offer an opportunity to head up a great project. This is the same scenario, two different potential realities.

Thought alert

Let's now look at the impact of our thinking and how it plays a huge part in all our responses. We can never stop our thoughts, that is a fact. In any situation, our minds are wired to find an association from within so that it can be interpreted. This is all done automatically. When our thinking is out of our awareness, it can run wild and cause havoc. We can feel very stuck, like we have no control and often are unable to move away from the past. Many of our automatic thoughts are recycled and associated with unhealthy self beliefs which ultimately holds us back.

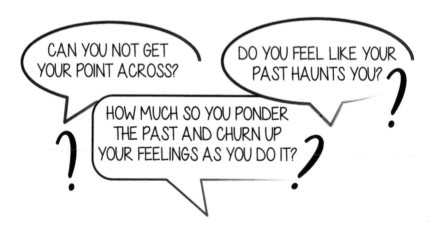

By becoming more aware of the actual thoughts then the interpretation can be challenged. Being more aware allows us to separate the unhelpful ones, rather than the impact of the interpretation taking the lead. Bang – the feeling of unhappiness or anxiety is there before you have had 'time to think'.

Stepping back and noticing exactly what your thoughts and feelings are, will be the start to changing yourself. As with meditation, stopping to notice your breathing gives you more control over it.

Becoming aware

The first task is to bring your awareness onto what kind of information is regularly in your thoughts. While reading this book, your mind will be constantly thinking, making associations and creating feelings, all relating to the words on the page.

Take some time now to notice and reflect on what kind of thoughts you have. What is on your mind? How you are feeling? Are you feeling inspired? Are you worried about something in your life? Are you annoyed or upset about an unfair situation? Or are you simply thinking about what's for dinner?

It is powerful to actually stop and write down whatever is on your mind, good or bad thoughts, formed or random and your emotions. Whatever is going around right now, then you can understand why we are not always getting what we want in life. When you become more aware of your thoughts and the quality of them, you can begin to have more control, by deciding what you will pay attention too. It is more common to just have thoughts running almost wildly without any order. But once you have noticed them, you can start to challenge or change them. We will work on this through the book together.

What are beliefs?

A belief can be created by a thought you have over and over again until it sits firmly as a truth in your subconscious mind. The initial thought however may have been based on something that may or may not have been true. It is worth noting that beliefs can also be created through an instant learning. For example, you get stuck in a lift and you believe that all lifts will stop when you get in them. The experience has made your thoughts about the situation become a truth.

We all have core beliefs which are things we believe are true about ourselves and the world, regardless of what anyone else thinks or feels. We will believe in them as long as we hold them in our mind. Beliefs can run our lives, and are often out of our awareness. Our choices, decisions, thoughts and behaviours can all be linked back to what we believe about ourselves and everything else in life. When we believe that we are a good person, our actions, responses and experiences tend to be in line with this belief, and therefore positive.

The opposite is true if we think we are a bad person; all experiences will be interpreted as if this were true. Complex beings, aren't we? These beliefs play a massive part in determining our reactions to situations and definitely to others' behaviour. When an idea is processed through the filters into the subconscious mind it may turn into a belief. In other words, when we hear something often enough, it becomes true. As children, we believe what a trusted source tells us. When we are told or say something often enough, it may then become a belief.

We are not consciously aware of many of the beliefs we hold. We all have our own values which are what are important to us and we will revisit these later in the book. Beliefs and attitudes developed throughout the course of our lives. Your family, friends, community and the experiences you have had all contribute to your sense of who you are and how you view the world. Many of these beliefs are positive, although watch out as the mind does keep hold of them all despite their quality.

If we have positive core beliefs, for example I am loved, and link them to ourselves, they become part of us simply because we think that way. We create our own reality of what we believe to be certain in our lives. Most of us know that we are good at some things. Some people can feel good about themselves much of the time because they have no problem keeping their focus on knowing that they are worthy.

Power of negativity

However, many of us have beliefs that inhibit our potential and therefore limit our choices. As mentioned previously, some core beliefs are created from our childhood and from past experiences. Unfortunately, these can be negative beliefs about ourselves. For example, it could start with a parent not knowing the impact of saying a child is stupid, clumsy or a nuisance. More often than not, these comments are said unintentionally and usually off the cuff. However, the subconscious mind takes everything very seriously, they can become a reality. The formation of a belief can even happen in jest, as a tease, or even with a look or other non-verbal messages which tells the child that they are wrong. Our subconscious mind then picks up clues and evidence that support this belief. It starts to interpret information to fit with the belief. The actual information is then distorted or even deleted. For example, if someone who received these messages as a child is rejected when they are older, a first thought could be, 'It's because I'm stupid'.

We construct our reality

Our beliefs are so powerful, they can direct us on our path of life. At the extreme, much of our self-concept, the Who am I? can be a mixture of several beliefs, both positive and negative. It almost becomes like a fiction based on these negative beliefs that are simply not true and can often overrule the good beliefs.

This mental image of ourselves develops from several routes, though is particularly influenced by our interactions with important people in our lives. It's these beliefs that drive us and such negative beliefs can totally ruin our lives to the point where we think we are a failure, not a good person, unlovable and can end up feeling like a victim.

In a positive way, we can believe that we are a smart or capable person. However, quite often the beliefs are limiting throughout an individual's life. A 70-year-old client of mine said that he had been told he was shy as a child; consequently, he had always been very anxious and awkward, and had had no close friendships or relationships because of his self-belief that he was shy. He had made this his reality and this had held him back throughout his life.

Henry Ford, an American industrialist and the founder of the Ford Motor Company, said "Whether you think you can or whether you think you can't, you are right." By forming these beliefs, we create a self-fulfilling prophecy, which is a positive or negative expectation of circumstances, events or people. It is when we unknowingly think in a certain way and then this causes an outcome.

This happens constantly. Some, obviously, can enable us in life although negative ones can disable us. A false belief is held as a truth.

For example, one day you may feel good about yourself and everything just seems to fall into place. Equally, have you ever woken up and just known that you were going to have a bad day? You then stub your toe, people at work are in a bad mood and negative things just seem to happen. This reinforces the idea we started with. It could be that you believe that you are unlucky or not a good person.

Another example is if you believe that you are going to fail an exam, or your new date is not going to like you, you will send out negative vibes. Regardless of how prepared you try to be, you are likely to receive what you don't want to happen.

Can you see how powerful your subconscious mind is in constructing your reality? 'Be careful what you wish for' could not be truer. We will be exploring how important it is to focus on what we do want to happen rather than on what we don't want to happen later.

Programmes and habits

Alongside the beliefs, our minds create programmes and habits about how we do things. We also create patterns in our thinking. Maybe you are a positive optimistic person or have a tendency to think negatively, always thinking the 'what if', for a situation. These programmes are developed over time and stored firmly in our subconscious mind.

If we think literally, each of us has a certain way that we do everything, such as the way we wash our hair. It becomes a habit. A pattern is developed and eventually we start to do things the same way without fail. We create or learn a habit of doing something and then we stick to that. This is great news for the good stuff although not so for the unhelpful habits.

A great example of how a habit is formed is when you learn to drive a car. At the beginning, you worry that you won't be able to do mirror, signal, manoeuvre at the same time, nevermind hold a conversation as well. This is because you are still using your conscious mind to drive. Once you are competent at driving, the auto pilot takes over and you can't remember stopping at traffic lights on the journey! Then you can drive without a lot of thought, singing to the radio or holding a conversation with someone. This happens because the driving habit has been transferred to the subconscious mind and so the conscious mind becomes free. A groove in your neural network is formed.

Once the information about driving is locked in the subconscious mind, it stores this as a programme. The mind is like a computer and the driving activity is like software which it run automatically. This happens for many other activities: riding a bike, brushing your teeth, putting your socks on. It is the same for our limiting behaviours when we are not reaching our true potential.

Buttons & triggers

Let's dig a little deeper into understanding what creates the responses and behaviours we have. Within our subconscious mind, it is as if we all have 'buttons' or 'triggers' which stimulate a response. As with anything, some are good reactions while others are not so good. Sometimes we can expect them for example, we know we are nervous giving a presentation, while others seem to come out of the blue.

For example, if you are unsure where you stand with a person and the second you see a text from them you get an emotional response. The automatic response can often be so instant that the trigger is completely out of your awareness. The subconscious mind is like the gate keeper, using the data stored from previous events to deduct likely probabilities and prompt us accordingly. Remember we have said before its primary job is to protect.

It is natural and necessary that we have a reaction to every trigger. The mind will be stimulated by everything external and it will find something from within to make sense to each of them. If, for example, as a child we believed we were unlovable, then any remark that reminds us of this unconscious wound will make us feel bad. It is these remarks that create firm, limiting self-beliefs which become a concrete part of us.

There is also a risk of misinterpretation; a person who believes he is stupid can interpret comments like, 'Why did you do that?' or 'What made you say that?' as reinforcement that he is stupid. Our mind will always gravitate to what it knows, not what is necessarily best for us.

Who is in control?

So, we have now established that our subconscious mind is powerful and can store everything, regardless of whether it is positive or negative, happy or sad. It is kept there in case it is needed for future reference. It is our very own 'Google' search engine. When we are aware of what lies underneath our responses, like our thoughts about ourselves, then we can start to switch our control. When we can be mindful of the natural emotional response to situations - such as nervousness, anxiety, sadness or anger - and understand what has driven it then we can change the impact.

We also know that the mind's intention is to look after us and often alerts us when a 'call to action' is needed. However, we can have a tendency to make communication and relationships difficult for ourselves when we have negative triggers which are out of our awareness. We can over complicate, confuse and interweave situations into mini crises. At a time of anxiety, upset or anger, we can feel out of control and consequently not make the best decisions.

As you progress through this book, you will learn that ultimately you can have more control more of the time - the trick is to work out the 'how'. With awareness and focus, you can start to control your thinking and ultimately your behaviour. You can drive your own bus!

Communication starts with you

It is fair to say that human communication and relationships are one of the most complex things in life. As incredible as we are, we are limited in our ability to truly understand others: why they do the things they do, why they say the things they say and what they actually mean. It can all feel like a mystery because we all process and interpret everything differently. The problem is we are often focused on other people and try to understand them. We often do this without an understanding of ourselves first. We need to learn how our own minds work before we start trying to decipher someone else's. It will help to remember that everyone is not thinking and feeling the same as you. Knowing this helps you to adjust your expectations.

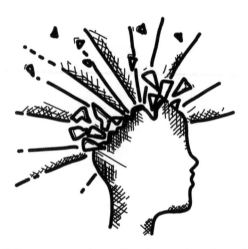

It is vital to remember that each of us is unique and that each person's 'map of their reality' is personal, intimate and incomparable to anyone else's. In order to understand our own world, we attempt to apply meaning and our own interpretation to other people's actions, behaviours and communications. We can get into 'sticky' territory because, quite simply, we all have our own way of doing things and yet expect the same from others. We will all have people that are more like us than others, although our minds work differently based on the information and interpretations of experiences.

We never truly know what is going on in someone else's mind and how they view the world. The trouble starts when we try to second guess what is going on for someone else. Mindreading and making assumptions is an area that we will be exploring further in the book.

Are you ready for the next step?

So, what have we covered so far? We have reviewed some theory about how the mind works and how powerful it is. We have compared the differences between the conscious and subconscious mind and have started to understand some of the functions. We know our responses are natural, constant and often expected - although not always helpful.

When we pay more attention to the type of thoughts we have and our behaviours, then we will have a greater chance of gaining more control. When we can spot that we are beating ourselves up, we know that painful old memories or limiting beliefs have taken centre stage. A common result of this is a display of highly emotional responses and an internal feeling of being unsettled, or just 'not right'.

In the next chapter, we will start to understand further what can influence us and what creates our internal map. We will look at what happens when we are still working with information that was created when we were younger, and how this can shape us as adults. We will delve deeper into how limiting beliefs and habits are formed and how these can keep us from our true path.

Let's continue on the journey of looking at our lives through a different lens and prepare ourselves to make the changes necessary to have the life we want. This can then become the new reality which will replace unhelpful behaviours and move us towards taking responsibility for our own destiny.

Just before you go, please consider the impact of the information you have so far. Quite often when we understand something, particularly the workings of the mind, it takes the pressure off as it starts to make sense. Hopefully this is true for you.

CHAPTER THREE

What SHAPES us?

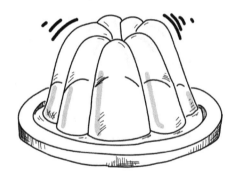

How our past experiences shape us

Now that we have an understanding of how the subconscious mind works , we can start to look at the kind of things that affect us and cause challenges! As we have explored the mind interprets, gets involved in, responds and has a feeling for literally everything. This is clearly a good thing although it is fair to say that this isn't always a positive experience.

Let us now delve a little further into our behaviours and consider what can influence us, which then affects our responses. In this chapter, we will explore what shapes or moulds us as individuals. It will help us to understand where many parts of ourselves, our challenges and difficulties stem from, but not forgetting our good traits! When we understand ourselves better, we can then make sense of situations and this can lead to change. Whether you have a question like 'Why is my life heading in this direction?' or 'Why doesn't my life feel quite right', we can start to find answers. Like any map, you need to know where you are before you can find another place.

It is true that all our lives will have had lots of positive situations and experiences. We also know that everyone is challenged at times. In fact, it would be very dull if everything went to plan, and how would we grow as individuals without a balance between good and challenging experiences?

Some situations in life are unavoidable and inevitable. While others seem out of our control, like they are 'done to us'. It is these latter situations which cause the most distress and dissatisfaction. When this happens we can get diverted by blaming someone else or a situation and therefore get stuck.

In adult life, with some situations it is obvious why we feel unhappy. Something has happened that was difficult to manage, cope with or has triggered a warranted emotional response, like a bereavement or accident. It is often harder to understand when we feel out of balance, stuck or blocked without a particular event or reason. It can be confusing to understand why a response is happening and what part we are playing in it. It can feel like it is happening 'to you' and can play out in many different and diverse ways. Many of us spend years looking externally for the answers, yet there are a wealth of rich answers within.

Here on our journey together, we will focus on influences and influencers. So may seem harmless and yet can have a negative (and even a destructive) impact. Once you are clearer on what can cause difficulties, then there are opportunities to make changes and take control of your life.

It's important to remember that we are not our problems. We all have internal challenges - which are sometimes explained and other times not. We often can't name them and they can be a mixture of emotions, behaviours, habits and thoughts. Our 'stuff' can feel like it defines us and, whatever it is, it tends to take over our lives.

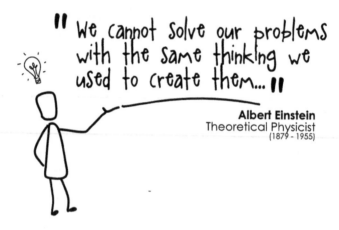

" We cannot solve our problems with the same thinking we used to create them... "

Albert Einstein
Theoretical Physicist
(1879 - 1955)

For example, if you struggle with anxiety it may affect you in many areas of your life. You don't feel like you have any control. This becomes your reality and you feel defined by it. This is not necessarily true, unless you let it. We wouldn't introduce ourselves as, 'Hi, my name is Anxious' or 'Hi, I'm Insecure'. It is this 'stuff' which can be changed. That's the good news!

Our childhoods

Let's start at the very beginning. Childhood is unquestionably one of the biggest influences for us all. It doesn't matter what you have experienced, it is fair to say we are all a product of our past and how this affects us is different for everyone. Much of what happened when we were children is usually apparent and shows up in our adult lives in some form or another. This can still be affecting us in the present day. It is interesting to note that things that happened in the past need not be traumatic events to have had an impact.

In the early years, through our experiences we learn about ourselves and the world from our caregivers and the people with whom we have contact. As babies and toddlers, we simply accept everything we are told. This is because young children only have a subconscious mind and part of its function is to believe everything, as the logical, rational mind is not yet developed. A benefit of this is that young children are in a gorgeous place of possibility. They don't doubt or question like an adult, are unable to connect things together and therefore are blissfully unaware of the consequences or the impact of their behaviour. They live in that free world of believing in everything, including themselves.

It is believed that the subconscious mind is shaped between the ages of zero to seven and the information learnt at this time is accepted to be true. This is literally everything you hear, from learning and recognising 'this is a table' to taking on board others' comments as mentioned earlier, such as 'you are loved' or 'you are stupid'. This information comes from many different sources and, from both verbal and nonverbal communication. Even that look your parent or teacher gave you will have had an effect.

All experiences start to develop the child in many ways. The beliefs, decisions and ideas about themselves start to form. From the very beginning, we never stop programming our subconscious mind. As children become more aware of the outside world, they will decide whether to accept or fight what they are experiencing. What they learn and accept becomes a basic part of their permanent character structure. Children generally communicate through emotions. Some will bury the emotions deep within, which may become a way of survival, while others are more expressive from the outset.

From this very early age, we begin to create our own personal map of reality and this continues throughout life. Each map is unique, never more apparent than when children are brought up by the same parents yet turn out with major differences in personalities and behaviours. Their experience of childhood is often described very differently, which drills home the huge differences with how each mind interprets experiences.

Changing the map of reality

There are many factors that affect our personalities and here we are only going to look at some of them. It is interesting to notice how differently people interpret situations. Any new experience will either reinforce the map of reality or alter it significantly. For example, if you have normally done well at school and you then pass your driving test first time, your map of your reality reinforces the evidence in the map that you do well. Some other experiences, on the other hand, can do the opposite and go against the evidence in the map and lead you to a different conclusion.

The map may have started out as holding certain evidence, like 'I don't make friends easily', and then you start a new college, where you very quickly make a friend in your class. This experience doesn't agree with your original map of reality. The map constantly changes and updates automatically. This usually happens out of your awareness. This, of course, is great with good experiences, but can cause problems when the negative 'evidence' dominates. The map is continually being reinforced throughout life and the response can become the norm.

It is understandable that we are affected by anything and everything that happens in life - good and bad, positive and negative. We are affected in some way by everyone, although much is out of our awareness and may be not even an issue. What we are interested in is how they have influenced and created an impact. Many of these influences are unavoidable and part of how we develop. We can learn from each other and choose to adapt ourselves.

Some influences happen without us realising. It just happens and we often don't take the time to step back and notice these things. Some actions of others are deliberately harmful, while others are often not intentional or done with malice. Through life we are constantly updating, adapting and developing our behaviours and thought patterns as a response. Many of these influences are healthy and have a positive impact, while others can be detrimental and more destructive. We all know this but it's worth taking time to notice the difference and to know that all are necessary for us to evolve and develop.

Parenting

There are many influences on us throughout our childhood, including society, family dynamics or our environment. There is the big debate of nature versus nurture. Some think that your personality is based on genetic predispositions - nature - pre-wiring influenced by genes and other biological factors.

Others conclude that nurture is the predominant factor - the way we act stems from the influences of external factors, life experience, the way we were taught, and the environment in which we grew up. The nature versus nurture debate will go on and on.

Whichever you believe, it is accurate to say our upbringing has a big impact on how we are moulded. Initially, we are affected by the people who cared for us, as well as other family members.

Then we become influenced by our friends, our friends' parents, our siblings' friends, work colleagues, intimate relationships and adult friendships. All these relationships shape us throughout the years and, of course, we ourselves are influencers in other people's lives.

Most children living in the UK have their basic needs met in terms of food, shelter, education and experiences. Where the difficulties can lie is often in the emotional and psychological support, sometimes in the way love and affection is shown. This is vital when we are forming our identity. However, when this support is missing, it often results in someone not knowing who they are and lacking belief in themselves. When any of our emotional needs are not met, the outcome is that we unconsciously feel unworthy.

" Are we born this way, or do we behave according to our life experiences?... "

Our parents' responsiveness plays a key role in our learning to communicate our complex inner lives to others. The ability to reflect on our own feelings, thoughts and needs and to understand those of others lays the groundwork for future relationships. When this is lacking as a child, it can cause difficulties within adult relationships, mainly because we don't know how to give or receive affection or to manage our emotions. For example, we can feel empty within relationships; we can believe our role is to 'show up' for others and so disregard our own needs. We can find ourselves wondering whether we are worthy of love, care or happiness. These can be long lasting, but the good news is that they are not set in stone for the future.

Different experiences throughout life will affect confidence, self-esteem and self-worth – all things that are vital to be your best, be your true self and follow your own path. Some children have been treated with explicit love and respect and are more likely to have a high level of self-esteem, confidence and an attitude of 'I can achieve anything'.

Others, on the other hand, have experienced less apparent love, belief, and even physical contact, which affects how they then see themselves - generally resulting in lower self-confidence and self-esteem.

These differing parental styles can have a major influence on how each child's map of reality is formed. Parents are usually mirroring how their childhood was and how they were parented. However, it is important to understand how and what we have been influenced by so we can make changes where needed.

We all know families who show love and affection freely, unconditionally and naturally. How we all show our love is usually similar to the way it happened to us, unless we break the mould. Many parents can actively show not just love but encouragement, praise, respect and support to their children and to each other. The child clearly knows that their parents are proud of them and believe in them – all vital ingredients for a self-assured adult.

We also know parents whose approach is more critical, more focused on what isn't going so well, or showing less physical or emotional affection. Remember it is often learned from the way they were parented, and this is the approach which is familiar to them. A parent would rarely willingly hurt a child; their intentions are good, and they are doing what they think is right. Some parents believe that having a lot, if not all, of the control with their children is the only way to go. When a parent has too many ideas about how their child should run their life, particularly once an adult, then they are likely to head for problems. Any teenager is going to need to stretch out into their own world and make choices (both good and bad) to find themselves.

How love was shown

It is worth just checking we understand the differences between unconditional and conditional love and how each can affect someone's approach to life. This helps us to understand what shapes us and how this influences our own relationships.

Unconditional love is more likely to be when a person is shown love simply for being who they are, regardless of what they do or haven't done. In a nutshell, I love you and nothing else you do will ever change that. In most cases, having unconditional love as a child brings joy, develops self-esteem, self-worth, confidence and allows the child to explore, grow and develop naturally. Most people who have been brought up with unconditional love are more likely to have learned to accept themselves for who they are and are happy being them. A simple example would be when a child or young person has not done as well as expected in their exams and the parents are supportive and talk about being proud of them regardless of the results.

The opposite is conditional love. This can often be linked to performance and behaviour. For example, if we live up to our parents' expectations and please them, then they will show us love. The downside is that love is withheld if we don't live up to their expectations. Love can become a weapon, or a dangling carrot associated with the child's success or failure. Love is given 'only if you do this...' which can be interpreted as 'If you don't do it, I don't love you'. However, this focuses on the negative and is often fear-based, with love seeming like something that must be earned. This sounds very black and white and it is probably better to think of it as more of a scale with a big grey area in the middle.

One of the obstacles to a child's success and happiness is when parents use their conditional love to threaten and control them. This often results in adults with lower self-worth, limiting beliefs, feelings of inadequacy and insecurity. The underlying message they have heard is 'You are not really good enough'.

With some people, conditional love can have a positive impact. It can lead to a highly productive and motivated adult because they will always try their hardest in order to receive praise for doing well. This does appear to be a good attribute, though problems can arise because the self-esteem is connected with the external factor of the other person. If they are unable to do something well, or fail, they will be hard on themselves and this can affect their self-esteem and confidence. They will associate failing with being a bad person, who is not worthy of being loved or liked.

Only success can allow them to feel a sense of belonging and acceptance from the significant people in their life. There can also be instances when it can cause paralysis; a fear of not doing something well causes them to not even try. Someone can adopt a 'Why do I even bother?' attitude. We will be looking at the harsh inner critic in the next chapter and learn that we don't have to always believe or follow our inner voice.

Just to ensure we have covered all bases, being loved unconditionally has its downside too. There are some situations where a child may have been done a disservice by their parent accepting everything is ok and challenging nothing. When a parent has never seen anything as being wrong, has ignored negative behaviours and is in denial that mistakes were made, including deliberate ones, there will be issues. The impact could be that as adults they have no idea how to be accountable or responsible and their ability to assess risk or see the impact of their behaviour is limited.

It is common that we behave as we have been shown. Most people parent as they were parented - although this is not an exact science. It comes down to how aware we are of our behaviour. Some people parent in the same loving way they were brought up; some were over-protected so may become overprotective parents. If someone was shouted at or even hit, there is a chance they will copy this behaviour, although not a given. When criticism is the primary mode of communication, they are likely to parent similarly.

Our parents are our first role models, and in fact our first managers too! When parents are absent as a role model, then a child will seek a substitute, often their grandparents, another family member or a significant adult in their life.

We will look a little more at the pros and cons of praise when we talk about communication later in this chapter.

The impact of our early experiences will show up in our daily behaviours, although commonly are out of our awareness. Parents often catch themselves sounding and responding like their own mother or father. For some, becoming like their parent is not an issue as theirs was a positive experience. For others, there is a fear, certainly in terms of mirroring the negative behaviour seen and witnessed. The trick is to notice which behaviours, values and attitudes you want to keep and those from which you would prefer to break free.

STEP to CHANGE

What has influenced you?

What has influenced you?

Take a moment to think about your own situation.

Consider at least three things that have influenced you in a positive way

Positive Influences

WHAT   HOW does this influence you?

1.

2.

3.

What do you believe about yourself?

Now consider at least three things that have influenced you in a negative way. Examples can include: past experiences, fear of the unknown, lack of self worth and low self esteem.

Negative Influences

WHAT   HOW does this influence you?

1.

2.

3.

What do you believe about yourself?

Software update

As humans we are continually changing and updating each time we are exposed to new situations, information and experiences. The aim is to make good changes although this is not always the case. The good news is once we are aware of any negative behaviours learned throughout our childhood, we can reject or replace them with a new and different approach. For example, a person that has been brought up in an emotionally cold environment can choose to be openly loving, although this is no mean feat.

UPDATE:......

As children we can have hopes and dreams which may not have our parents' approval. Children are natural dreamers and should be encouraged to express and use their imaginations. This develops confidence, self-belief and supports the decision-making process later in life. When we share our desires yet receive negative feedback we can learn to deny or disown these feelings to please our parents. The result is an adult who puts their own needs second to those of others.

There is also the impact of our influencers having their own limiting beliefs. Parents will have ideas, hopes and dreams for their children, though this can be based on their own capacity and capability. Some parents push and encourage their children to do all the things they didn't have the chance or confidence to do. While others hold them back, not necessarily on purpose, just seeing things through their own doubt or fears. A limiting view from a parent is likely to be associated with their own map of their reality. Parents are generally driven to protect their child from anything that they believe is dangerous and guide them accordingly. However, there can be instances where perceived danger is anticipated because the parent couldn't imagine doing it themselves. For example, discouraging a child from going travelling because the parent believes it is unsafe. This can cause conflict and there is a risk that the child's path in life is being influenced by someone else's fears and uncertainty.

We live in a competitive society, so it's no surprise that parents feel pressure for children to compete and excel. Many parents want their children to be perfect, which is unrealistic, and this can cause anxiety and disappointment all round.

As we have established, the creation of negative self-limiting beliefs starts within childhood and is inevitable. This can happen as a result of the child being unsure how and what they need to do to please their parents. When a child believes that they are unable to please their parents, they are less likely to be satisfied with results unless they are 100% perfect. This causes problems as there are very few occasions in life when it is realistic to expect this kind of achievement. In adulthood, a pattern of seeking perfection is developed or a natural stance of being hard on themselves evolves.

Expectations

A positive situation is when parents can have a set of realistic expectations for their children which sends a powerful message that they care and believe in them regardless.

There are some scenarios when parents have low expectations and don't expect enough: the child loses confidence in their abilities to achieve. They can show signs of anger, anxiety and sadness. The opposite can also be true. A parent can have an idea of what the child should do and may push them in a direction that is not right for them. There is no blame here although this can change the course of someone's life, be wrong for that person and lead to resentment.

At this point, it's important to highlight that this book is mainly to help you understand the path you are on and how that differs to the path you want to follow. If you are a parent, this is not intended to create paranoia about everything you say to or do with your children. It is simply to raise awareness and understand why we are like we are as adults. Children don't come with a manual and each child, even in the same family, is unique and therefore experiences life differently. Most of us do the best we can with the tools we have. Bare this in mind when considering any relationships, rather than jumping to blaming others, especially parents.

People act with their best intentions and basically the only way they know. Acknowledging this helps to take the pressure off and encourages you to look for a different approach. Each child can 'need' different things, depending on who they are and how they have interpreted each experience. For example, giving constant feedback could be needed by one child and another prefers to be left alone as they can reassure themselves. These types of differences will usually play out later in life too. It is fascinating to notice these differences within families and highlights how unique we all are.

Everyone has a story about their own childhood. We talk about how it was, how we felt, what the relationship is like now and how we behave with our parents as adults. This story and our perception continually changes over time too.

Blaming parents or anyone else for our own struggles keeps us stuck in anger, anxiety and sadness. This interferes with our ability to think about what we could do to make our lives different. For example, difficulties like insecurities or fearing rejection in relationships could be blamed on a parent's emotional coldness, criticisms, or their own unhealthy relationship. Another is blaming a parent's lack of encouragement and involvement when growing up for their own failure to do well academically or professionally. While blaming is fruitless, what is important to highlight is that our experiences will affect how we are. It is these behaviours that we can change for ourselves to be happier in our lives. Acceptance and forgiveness play a huge part in moving forward and we will come onto that later.

Siblings

It is fascinating why siblings are so different to each other, even when they are raised in the same family environment. In addition to genetic differences, competition between siblings can affect their development. Our social and communication skills are developed as we learn to negotiate and influence within the family unit.

There has been a lot of research about how adult behaviour has been influenced by the birth order in families (being the eldest, middle or youngest child), or being raised as an only child, as well as other dynamics such as stepchildren and blended families. As this topic could be a whole book in itself, we will merely acknowledge some of the factors which shape us in relation to the position held in the birth order. Our birth order can affect our emotions, behaviour and personality development.

The position in which we are born within the family will create unique emotional experiences. You obviously can't change your birth order, although when there is an acknowledgement of the possible impacts and influences, then you are empowered to not be disadvantaged to the challenges. For a first child, there can be feelings of empowerment, having been emerged in love and security. However, there can also be high expectations of them because of the level of attention, and they can be prone to stress from self-imposed pressure for accomplishment. There can also be feelings of loss and even jealousy when a new child arrives. Their nurturing skills can lead them to be loving and sensitive to other people's needs.

A middle child can also feel jealous due to their sibling accomplishing new firsts. They can feel invisible and left out. This can lead to competitiveness and constantly trying to chase after the older sibling. As they grow up, they are neither the oldest or the youngest and this can lead to a struggle to establish their own identity.

The last born may grow up expecting others to take responsibility; they may be non-conformists and more free spirited. Gender, the number of years between each child, the relationship between the parents, loss of a parent, the absence of a parent and families blending together will undoubtedly contribute to the impact on a childhood.

Emotions

Humans are emotional beings. It is acceptable for young children to live with uncontrolled emotions. Children are forgiven for tantrums, strops, banging doors or locking themselves away, because they use emotions to communicate while their rational, sensible mind is still to mature. As adults it is expected that we 'grow up' and manage our emotions. Some people naturally are more demonstrative, while others are more guarded. Mastering and managing emotions also varies between us and this can often be linked to our childhood experiences.

In our adult life, we are continually trying to react to things in an appropriate manner. The human mind is wired to have feelings for everything and expressing them is perfectly acceptable.

There are a range of different emotions we express that make communication so interesting. Most of them could almost be put into two categories, love-based ones such as happiness, joy or fear-based ones such as anger and guilt.

The trick to grow is to notice what is triggering our uncontrolled emotional responses, which are taking over our lives. Sometimes this can stem from how we have been shown how to manage emotions and we are merely mirroring learnt behaviour. For example, a highly anxious parent will often bring up an anxious child. If we haven't been shown how to respond positively and have watched how adults attempt to gain control through emotions, then we will be unsure how to behave. This will be a stretch if we have been brought up in a highly emotional family situation or the opposite, where emotions were not shown at all.

Either way, we can learn to manage our emotions and our drama, both internally and externally, and this is certainly something to master as an adult. Otherwise there is a risk of being told to 'grow up' and things will simply continue not to go the way we want them too. Let's not waste time wishing your childhood had been different, just simply notice these traits so that you can make sense of yourself and your own behaviours.

Early instructions

Words are very powerful tools, and there are tips and ways of using words to improve relationships. A set of lovely positive words can have an immediate positive effect and can make someone feel joyous, confident, respected and happy. Equally, when used negatively, words can cause embarrassment, sadness or humiliation. There is a grey area, when words have been spoken and the influence is hidden.

The way adults talk to children is teaching them how to talk to others. Some parents and influential adults use an authority which doesn't necessarily allow the child an independent voice or sense of efficacy. Others can overcompensate with overly permissive parenting that doesn't teach the children about limits, boundaries and self-control. Both extremes affect the child's ability to regulate their emotions and to form healthy relationships as adults.

A simple example is when a child spills a drink on the carpet or is messy when eating their meal; they may be shouted at and called stupid. Even if something is an accident, we may still blame the child and give them a hard time. Humiliating or shaming a child can shape their mind pathways in a negative way. This method of communication suggests to a child that this is how they deserve to be treated, which is a message then carried into adulthood and plays out later in life.

Children are often raised with early instructions like 'No' and 'Stop' aimed clearly to keep them safe, as well as 'Don't do that' or 'Do what I say'. It is interesting how the young mind processes this. It is a parents' responsibility to guide their child through life, but if this is predominantly what they hear, it can make it very limiting. As they are being told what to do and what not to do, it can become confusing to understand who they are as individuals. This can result in the creation of limiting beliefs. If there is little autonomy while they learn, there will be little chance to make sense of themselves and develop their own thinking and emotional growth.

A few examples can be don't cry or don't cry in public could be interpreted as don't let your parents down; don't think; don't feel; don't be childish; don't be yourself; don't make mistakes; don't be too concerned about yourself; don't put your own interests before others; don't stand out and be noticed; or don't show off. A child takes these messages into their subconscious mind and the impact can be highly negative.

It goes without saying, compliments, positive feedback and self-belief all contribute to feeling content and happy. Children develop a sense of competence by seeing the consequences of their actions, less so by being told about the consequences of their actions. When there isn't any feedback, or they are being told what to do or think it can lead to doubt and believing that they are not enough. This stays with them in adult life.

Praise

Encouragement is a vital part of human need for most. The question is what kind of encouragement is being given and how it is received. Most adults use praise to encourage and reward their children, although inappropriate praise can be harmful, just like criticism. Research has shown that how we praise our children has a powerful influence on their development. When children are praised for their intelligence, compared to their effort, they can become overly focused on results. Following a failure, these same children persisted less, showed less enjoyment, attributed their failure to a lack of ability (which they believed they could not change), and performed poorly in future achievement efforts. Praising children for intelligence makes them fear difficulty because they begin to equate failure with stupidity.

Let's have a quick look at the different types of praise and how they have a different impact. There is generalised praise, such as saying 'Well done', which is not wrong; however, this does not give any specifics, so this can be ineffective as the child doesn't know what to replicate. Exaggerated praise such as 'You did the best job in the world' can cause the child to be worried because they know that the praise doesn't match up to what they have done. This type of praise is often ignored as the child becomes aware that it doesn't represent the reality. As an adult, this may result in rejecting any form of praise and they can find it hard to accept a compliment. When we praise a child for absolutely everything they do, the impact as an adult is that they constantly seek approval for everything and become upset or rejected when they don't receive praise. This can develop a deep-rooted belief that they don't deserve the praise. It's good to think about this for yourself and help explain some of your own behaviours.

Criticism

Another obvious statement is that no one likes being criticised, just like we don't want to be told what to do. Negativity is like Velcro which sticks to us and overwhelms us, whereas positivity is like Teflon and slides right off!

Unconstructive criticism has a devastating effect on our self-esteem. If as a child we were frequently criticised, we quickly learn to self doubt. A self-limiting belief is formed that we are incapable of getting anything right, which leads to problems of self-worth and confidence. It is also common to see self-sabotaging behaviours that limit achievement and success in the future. We can then become our own worst enemy. We have been trained to be negative, see or fear the worst. Our inner critical voice forms throughout our early life experiences and often, without realising, we internalise comments and attitudes from our parents or care givers.

STUPID... WRONG!
RUBBISH UGLY! CLUMSY

For example, if a parent calls their child lazy or useless, they may grow up feeling useless or ineffective and engaging in self-sabotaging thoughts such as 'Why bother trying?'; 'You'll never succeed anyway'; 'You just don't have the motivation to get anything done'. This can develop into an emotional wound that lasts for a lifetime.

Another simple example is when a parent repeatedly says that their child is clumsy, the child is likely to become even clumsier and have regular mini accidents - spill their drinks and knock things over. They are subconsciously believing and becoming what they are hearing. The negative reaction from the parents reinforces the beliefs and so it goes on. When children get criticised in a way that makes them feel worthless, they might question their parents' love. It may feel like the conditional love we talked about earlier. Spending a childhood 'trying' to get it right and yet being told that we are wrong can be damaging. It may feel like we can never please our parents.

Rejection

As humans our need to belong is vital to our existence. Rejection of any kind therefore will hurt us and is probably something most of us dread. It is fair to say that most of us will naturally seek (and even yearn) parental interest, approval and attention even as an adult. Technically, we are always the 'child' in this dynamic. Winning parental approval is something that seems to give us safety and security. This approval can be a powerful influence on our behaviour. We may be highly successful in our own lives and yet still find ourselves hurt if a parent appears to not be interested or is critical of us and our choices.

Earlier we explored the difference between conditional and unconditional love. In some families there can be what appears to be 'the favourite' or the 'golden child' who seems to be treated differently. This can be related to birth order.

This may be true, although sometimes happens unintentionally. In some instances, it is an internal feeling or belief rather than a reality. Remember that the mind can process things incorrectly. This affects self-worth and beliefs and may be interpreted as rejection. It can result in a child thinking: 'I don't get noticed', 'I'm not special', 'no one listens to me', or 'I can't seem to get anything right'.

These kinds of experiences can create a fear of rejection and this can then play out in our other relationships. It can even happen in a business relationship, when a boss's behaviour may be like a parent, and it will certainly happen in intimate relationships. There can be a huge dread that the other person is going to reject us, which can breed insecurity and create challenges in a relationship, particularly a new one.

Still a child?

It's interesting to observe our relationships with our parents once we are an adult. We can often still feel like a 'child', almost reverting back to being a six-year-old sometimes. In some cases, we become great friends with our parents and being with them is still fun. Some have a relationship where we can reach out, feel supported and can lean on them. In other situations, we can feel like we are being treated like a child who has no voice or acknowledgement of our decisions as there is always a comment - often a negative comment!

Some parents still have or appear to want to have some control or feel the need to criticise an adult child. This is clearly not ideal and will have a negative effect. As an adult, we can be driven by the child-like memory that we can't get anything right. This is the internal filters at work and the responses created are based on our map of reality. This type of constant criticism makes you believe that there is something wrong with you and can lead to feelings of shame. It might force a person to become socially withdrawn, fearful of expressing their emotions or taking risks. This can play out in adult life in a variety of ways which we will explore later.

Not feeling seen or heard

We all know the old Victorian saying, 'Children should be seen and not heard'. While times have moved on somewhat, there are still instances when a child is unable to express themselves or experiment with their own emotions. This can make them feel stifled and frustrated. When a child is developing their identity, let alone personality, it is vital that they are encouraged to be free and be themselves. Young children tend to do this well and then, as the conscious mind develops, embarrassment, doubt and uncertainty kicks in. This is normal and natural, but some reactions can exacerbate the situation. An example could be when a child is not able to talk about their feelings, as feelings are not discussed within a family. Instead, they are told how to feel, maybe because the adult is minimising the response to a situation and therefore the child is left feeling confused.

Some parents reject their child's desire to be seen, heard and understood without realising. People who have lived with this often grow up with a sense of not feeling important or special. An example of this would be a child running up to a parent full of joy, and then angrily being told to shut up and go away, or maybe a teenager wants to talk about a difficult relationship and they are told, 'Don't worry about it,' or, 'Things like this happen'.

The result of this is that the child craves to feel visible. This affects the development of self-esteem and confidence. They may be afraid to express their emotions or thoughts for fear of not being listened to or taken seriously. This then forms self-limiting beliefs such as 'I am not worthy to speak' or 'Nobody is interested in me'. This most certainly will play out in future relationships.

Influencers

We have been exploring some of what and who can have an impact on us as children. Along with our parents, there are a raft of people who will have had an impact throughout our life. They all shaped us as we became an adult. We will know who our influencer(s) in life have been, though stopping to think about how they have influenced us, can give us answers and reflections on why we are like we are. It's good to spend time noticing both the good stuff as well as the things that appear 'bad', as these can be turned into positives in the end.

Spend some time identifying who have been the biggest influencers on your life from both angles, positively and negatively.

STEP to CHANGE

Who has influenced you?

Who has influenced you?

Take a moment to think about your own situation.

List three people who have had a positive influence on your life:
(e.g. someone who helped you believe you were capable of doing
something) and then reflect on the way in which these people
have influenced you.

Positive Influencers

Name   How has this person influenced me?

1.

2.

3.

Now list three people who have had a negative influence on your life (e.g. someone who criticised you).

Negative influencers

Name   How this person influenced me?

1.

2.

3.

Identity

The easiest way to explain identity is our own sense of self. For example, your identity may be that you are a female who is honest, warm, caring, intelligent, and sometimes moody! This identity tends to show up in all areas of life. The way you perceive yourself, your actions, your thoughts and your interactions with others are all influenced by this identity. Your identity could be I am a mother, but who are you when you are being 'a mother' and what does society say you should be doing as a mother?

We obviously all have many roles within the family. It could be a mother, father, husband, wife, son, daughter, brother, sister, auntie, uncle, grandparent etc. We have a role in other environments too. We are a pupil or student; we are a friend, a neighbour, a colleague or a partner. All these roles shape our identity.

Families are not democracies. Each family has its own way of organising itself. It is common for the parents to have the power and authority within the unit and which rights, privileges, obligations and roles are assigned to each member. In most families, parents are expected to be the leaders and children are expected to follow this leadership. This shapes many aspects of our ability to be managed and lead within a work context, and ultimately how we are as a leader.

Within the unit, different family members can take on different responsibilities, like an emotional one or a director. These roles are then carried through to adulthood and form part of your identity. Do any of the following roles ring true for you? Hero (perfect child), Scapegoat (problem child), Dreamer, Mascot (Funny/CarefreeChild), Rescuer (fixer/problem solver) or Carer (looks for everyone else).

As you can see, some of these roles are positive, others are a survival role to cope with the situation within the family. Many of these roles are then transferred to relationships outside the family dynamic which may not be appropriate, and it can be difficult to break these old patterns.

As you work towards understanding what has influenced your own life, take time to reflect on the roles that you played in your own younger years. This will help you to identify traits and roles that you adopt or are given within your adult life.

STEP to CHANGE

Your role in your family

Your role in your family

Take a moment to think about your situation.

Consider if you had/have an emotional role within your family or friendships and note down what behaviours you displayed.

MASCOT

HERO

DREAMER

SCAPEGOAT

RESCUER

CARER

Social self and true self

With these family roles in mind, it is interesting to explore the impact of others' expectations, their opinions and how much these affect our actions. This can cause a challenge between what we will call your social self, who wants to please others and will do what you 'should' versus the real you.

It is very common to be concerned by what others think of us. In fact, we are governed by what others expect of us. This can be another reason why we get on the wrong life track. These situations can lead to feeling insecure, stifled, trapped, confused and often lonely because we are not following our own path. An example could be everyone is saying that you should finish school, do 'A' levels and then go off to university. By living up to other people's expectations, you could be completely on the wrong path.

Because of the impact of other people's opinions and an innate desire to not upset anyone, we often ignore our own needs and hopes. We are so often driven by society's expectations of us and this is shaped by what we think others think or expect of us. For example, you might find yourself wanting to get married because that is what is expected of you and yet this may not be what you truly want.

How often do we find ourselves in conflict with our social self and our true self? People can be nervous or unsure about their own future because it appears to be different to what is considered the 'norm'. But what is 'normal'? What can be right for one person is certainly not right for all. It can feel like we 'should' be doing what is expected. We can feel bombarded by so many different influencers telling us what is acceptable in our life and these include our families, friends, the media, and society in general.

This can be for literally any decision we want to make about our lives. It could be in relation to a career path, having children, who you want to be in a relationship with, where you live – there will always be someone who has an opinion which doesn't fit with your ideas. While it is ok for people to have their opinion, what we are interested in here is whether this has been pushed onto you and ultimately changed your decisions.

Do these situations stimulate an emotional response in you which triggers your own doubt, shame, guilt, or anxiety? The question is, do the feelings come because you are too nervous to follow your own true path (which may feel scary - in a good way) or because you are doing the opposite to what society and others expect you to do? This can emerge as a conflicting voice in your head, creating confusion and stress. Quite often we become indecisive or maybe we start to feel different from the 'norm'. This can prevent you from doing what is right for you and you follow the masses!

Self-limiting beliefs

Many of the beliefs you hold are positive, healthy, and good ones. They allow you to succeed and come with a good feeling. Positive beliefs are linked to your self-confidence and self-worth. It is these positive beliefs that drive you forward to going for what you want and finding a way to achieve it.

It is more important to know what your positive beliefs are as they create resilience and power. We all have lots of positive behaviours and habits that fill our lives and yet we have a tendency to focus on the negative things. The positive ones are almost in the background because we will be focused on what we can't do, and we seem to go to the default button of thinking negatively about ourselves. Our goal is to create more positive beliefs that will then override the unwanted ones.

It is vital to reiterate that all beliefs will be affecting the path of life. Believing that you can or can't do something will drive life and it is the 'can't' ones that hold us back. We have identified that these beliefs can be formed partly because of others' opinions, comments, and actions which we interpret to be negative towards us. The reality is we all have some limiting beliefs in one form or another. This may be a deep-rooted question such as: 'Am I good enough?' 'Am I worthy?' or 'Am I lovable?'

The impact of having any limiting beliefs varies. They can be much more obvious in some people's lives than others. Commonly, confidence and trust will be affected. We also know that limiting beliefs can be created at any time in life and, unless they are addressed, can become more of a problem. Beliefs will continue to be reinforced by situations or a new belief can be formed by new experiences. The type of internal thinking, behaviours and how we respond to others are all indicators that the beliefs are running the show.

I now invite you to take some time to think about what you believe about yourself currently. You now know some of the reasons you can have limiting beliefs about yourself. It is good to be honest with yourself and acknowledge what is happening in your life. Remember, many of these limiting beliefs are not always obvious as they can be running in the background.

STEP to CHANGE

Your self beliefs

Your self beliefs

Take a moment to think about your situation.

Without judgement or blame, be honest about your own self beliefs. By spending time on this exercise, you can start to be less hard on yourself.

POSITIVE Self beliefs

Examples of positive beliefs may be that: I am confident, I am capable or I am lovable.

1

2

3

4

5

6

NEGATIVE Self beliefs

Examples of negative beliefs include: I am not good enough, I am stupid or I am unlovable.

1

2

3

4

5

6

By being honest and naming your negative or limiting beliefs, you now have information as to why you respond to situations in certain ways. It makes so much more sense when you are aware and can understand what is behind your behaviours. When you can see why you react in certain ways, it takes the pressure off. You can stop being hard on yourself, which is counterproductive, because you can see why. You are then able to make changes and have more peace and happiness in your life.

Comfort zone

Once you are aware of your own limits, you can notice how they are holding you back. They become your norm and these norms become your comfort zone. The thought of pushing yourself can feel uncomfortable - so you don't. You don't know any different and often say something like, 'it has always been like this'.

An unwillingness to move out of your comfort zone blocks potential and growth. You can get stuck and believe that you can't seem to do anything about your situation. You are stuck in the past. Life can feel uncontrollable and you don't know how to change it. Even though a situation is negative, often painful or creating unhappiness, it is common to stay in these situations because it is just how it is. The pattern is unaddressed, for example, you continue to be treated badly by a family member or a partner and do nothing about it.

Without realising, we are all limiting ourselves in one way or another rather than taking steps to a better future. To make the right changes takes courage. Another path often feels unachievable because we are usually in the emotional part of the mind and therefore unable to see new possibilities.

In some instances, old habits and behaviours which used to work effectively when you were younger often become redundant and unhelpful. They may be unhelpful now although they were a coping strategy once. For example, being invisible as a child may have worked to keep yourself out of trouble, but as an adult this approach would leave you feeling lonely and likely to be anxious to make friends or speak up for yourself.

Taking the past into your future

As you start to become much more aware of what exists within you and how your mind is wired to respond and protect you, you can create that much-needed instruction manual for your mind. When you notice your thoughts, feelings and how this all affects your behaviour, then you can move forward.

With everything that we understand now about our minds and our personalities, it is good to know that we can free ourselves from the past with careful guidance and self-care.

"Noticing your limiting beliefs, your doubts and assumptions, will help you see patterns in your behaviour..."

It is all too common to spend days, weeks, months and even years in some cases, chewing over the same kind of thinking. This is often related to someone or something that has happened, particularly when we believe we were hurt, let down or wronged. Dwelling on the past becomes a pastime. The energy and emotion that this takes up is draining and can harm us physically.

In her book , You Can Heal Your Life, author Louise Hay says, "The root of much disease is a negative attitude about taking care of ourselves".

Living in the past, regretting and feeling guilty only hurts, confuses and serves no purpose. It ultimately causes pain and discomfort. Believe it or not, the past can't hurt us, as it is gone. Yet we keep the memories alive in our minds as if we are constantly hitting the repeat button.

The mind will naturally live in the past if we allow it. We will look for someone else to blame rather than take action. We use the past as a weapon against others. We use the evidence from the past to justify or qualify our beliefs, particularly when there is conflict. It allows us to defend our position or blame another, all of which is only our perception and therefore not necessarily the reality. Remember the map of your reality.

It is fair to say that life will always throw up challenges and adversity. This adversity can act like a stop sign, or it can create a stronger character. Imagine life being like a sailing experience. Would we become a great sailor if the water was like a millpond? No, we become a skilled sailor when we go out in windy conditions. It is good to see life a little like this and be able to grow and expand from the challenges.

When you have a deeper understanding of how your family, culture and all your experiences have influenced you, your self-understanding can then develop. Your ability to make changes, both within yourself and in your relationships with others improves. By having a handle on 'why' things have happened, notice the tendency to go for the blame game, (which includes it not being your fault) and accept the part that you do play.

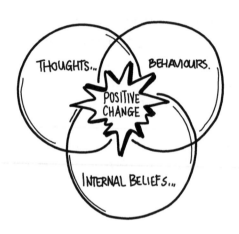

If your relationship with your parents, or in fact anyone else from your younger years, is fraught and you are still reliving it, you are harming yourself. You are the only one that can change the future. The power is within you. You can help yourself by changing your thoughts about what happened and notice the impact it is having on you personally. The other person often hasn't changed and, in some instances, can't or won't change. They may even be unaware and certainly not willing to take any responsibility.

We don't change because we grow up. We change when we become clearer about ourselves. As adults, it can feel like you have grown up on the outside and not on the inside.

This now takes us nicely into the next chapter – how it plays out - where we will explore the patterns and behaviours we adopt (usually unconsciously) and how they can impact on us. When you can take control of your own life, you can respond differently, start to learn from situations and work out how to be your own true self. The more you know about yourself, the more effective you can be, and the more comfortable you become in your own skin. We all know that knowledge is power, but self-knowledge equals self-power, which is limitless.

CHAPTER FOUR

Experiences & Expectations

We are ready now to start to look deeper at our thoughts and behaviours and how these drive and construct our lives. We have already explored how our mind processes and stores information and how this is used in the creation of a response. We will now be looking at some of the negative behaviours which we tend to develop. Common traits we all display. No one really escapes these behaviours seen day to day. In many instances, these are out of our conscious awareness. It is therefore helpful to spell them out and name them, bringing them into the awareness. Consider my belief that 80% of any change is being aware.

We have established that we can't stop thoughts. What is important is the attention we pay to them, particularly those of poor quality. It is good to stop and to notice what they are like. Quite often our minds are filled with negative or damaging thoughts which consume us and yet these are often out of our awareness. The thoughts come although what we do with them is what makes the difference. When negative thoughts go unnoticed, they can take over and affect our behaviours. Then we are likely to find ourselves stuck in a spiral.

This is important because our thoughts define us. When we notice our thoughts, we can make more sense of our lives. As we become aware of the link between what we think and what happens. Did you know that we don't have to always believe everything we think, particularly about ourselves, nor do we have to take action?

This chapter will encourage you to pay attention to the responses, especially checking in with any irrational emotional responses which then result in a range of unhelpful behaviours. When you witness yourself doing this, there is an opportunity to do something different, which will allow you to lead a happier and more fulfilled life.

Just as we continually breathe, we are continually 'updating' our internal world and thinking. This can unconsciously reinforce beliefs (especially limiting beliefs) about ourselves. Some of these behaviours may have been effective when we were young, though are often out-of-date and unhelpful later in life. For example, we can't have an emotional strop when we don't understand what we are feeling, like we did as a child. It's vital and valuable to be aware of your own patterns, beliefs and habits and then you can begin to make changes.

The auto responses

The first response to another person or a situation is likely to be an emotional one. Remember, the mind is wired to protect and work out 'is this ok?' or 'how do I feel about this?' It also makes a very quick check, an association between the current situation and any previous experience. While this is clever and natural to keep us safe, it can cause complications.

The mind thinks it is protecting you by alerting you that something is a potential threat, often a social threat. For example, a friend has asked to talk to you and you don't know why. It can trigger a negative emotion or memory of an experience associated with something similar, even slightly, that happened in the past. It automatically gives you a response, a feeling or a thought, which can be unwarranted in the now.

In most situations, we rarely stop to check the reason for our response; it just happens and most often we are focused on the actions of the other person and view it as some sort of personal attack.

There is a vast amount of neuroscience research which confirms that these responses are natural and associated with what each has stored inside. This helps us understand that people respond differently in situations. When we learn to step back, notice what and why it is happening, we gain valuable feedback. Taking a step back allows a complete change in perception of these situations and is like a fresh pair of eyes. These can become little 'gems' of feedback, your lessons in life, relationships and love, and it is these that will bring you closer to your own path and happiness.

We will explore the impacts of limiting beliefs, such as 'I am not good enough', 'I am not worthy', or 'I don't deserve' and explore the behaviours we are often exhibiting as a result. Some of these behaviours you will recognise as your own and some are displayed by others in your life. These negative behaviours become the norm, like a default position. As they are like 'auto-pilot', it can feel that there are no alternative options. Some of these common behaviours are similar and there is certainly a lot of overlap between them too. They can also occur simultaneously.

Re-sit class

Life is full of important lessons for us all - although we often don't get them first time, second time or even many times round (so termed the 're-sit class'). The re-sit class is where you find yourself in a similar or practically identical, unhealthy situation or relationship repeatedly. We all say we learn from our mistakes and yet often don't change any part of our behaviours.

We are often like Bill Murray in Groundhog Day, for those that remember that film, and have our own behaviours on repeat. An example is someone who has a limiting belief, exhausts themselves seeking other's approval and becomes burnt out. The message here is to spot the limiting belief and also to change the behaviour of overcompensating with others. This will only stop when you acknowledge your part. Alternatively, a number of people in your life behave in a certain way. For example, controlling or a drain to your resources and yet it seems to be out of your control. You are actually attracting them and this will continue until you are able to see your own behaviour.

The lessons clearly come in good, although mainly difficult experiences. Many things work out just as they are meant to and yet this isn't always a nice journey. We are often so stuck in our heads that we are unable to see what is best or why something is happening. The trick is to work out the messages or learning from these more difficult situations. Relationships with others are the most obvious environment for these challenges and thus lessons. If you don't pay attention, the lessons will be repeated until you do, or you can find yourself a victim of circumstance and you will re-visit the re-sit class! If you hear yourself thinking or saying 'Why does this keep happening to me' read on......

The first step

The first step is to notice if you are doing too much or not enough of something. Noticing this is valuable. What you are probably ignoring or not completely aware of is the important lesson. A word of warning, this takes courage admitting that your own behaviours are contributing to the difficulties. It is much easier to blame someone else.

Understanding and accepting the lesson out of the challenging situation will allow you to move on and grow. When you can see your 'mistakes' as information about you, then this allows you to make changes to be a better version of yourself. You can learn from every situation. We are so often focused on the details of the situation that has gone wrong - the people involved, the event, and therefore intuitively want to move away from it, fight it or become stuck. When we stop to notice that a situation or scenario hasn't worked out, we gain valuable information towards a new approach. This is feedback which is useful. When the thinking changes about a situation, you will be able to move out of the re-sit class with a new insight.

When you become open to life lessons, you can grow and become a better self. There is feedback to be gained on your own behaviours in most situations. This is obviously the case for us all even though some find it harder than others to accept. It is common to find yourself in the trap of blaming the other person when things go wrong. We are almost conditioned to do this.

There is subtle internal self feedback all the time on your own behaviours. An example could be that you are constantly tired and not looking after yourself because you can't stop yourself doing too much for someone else. The physical signal to yourself is that you are over tired, and the lesson is that the need to run around after others is unhealthy. When there is something not quite right, it is common to be either doing too much or too little of something.

These realisations usually mean that we need to give up on old behaviours as they are not giving us the results we want. For example, through a need to please and for acceptance, you may find yourself sharing too much in a new relationship. While sharing is good, you find yourself feeling vulnerable and resentful that you have shared so much. You could become annoyed with your partner and blame them that they 'made' you share or you can take the useful lesson that in the future you will be mindful of what you share about your past. It seems simple, although it is common to jump into a position of blaming the other person and staying annoyed with them. This behaviour will only drain you and fill you with negativity.

Patterns and habits

We have already mentioned how the mind creates habits and patterns. It is important to reiterate this as there is so much power in them.

When we want to make changes, first we need to be clear what changes are needed and which ones belong to whom. When we are unaware of our responses and actions, they are in a blind spot. From here, it is hard to spot how we have affected the situation and to be able to see what needs to be done. We have to catch ourselves and understand why it is happening so we can change it. We can't change what we haven't spotted.

Our lives are full of behaviour patterns (you could call them habits). They are familiar to us and so become the norm. Many are obviously positive and are a huge part of how and who we are, while others can cause us pain and suffering.

Imagine all these habits create a 'groove' in our neural network, which leads us in the same direction time and again. This includes what we do and how we do it. We have patterns in our thinking, these become habits too. On a basic level, as mentioned earlier, have you noticed that you will put your shoes and socks on exactly the same way every time? We do so many things in a particular way without any conscious thought as it is built in as a habit.

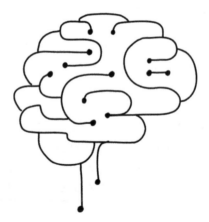

We can have instant thoughts which are a habit in themselves. We can have the same thought every time about a person or situation. This can feel so strong it is immovable. For example, a person can think that people driving a red car are flashy or that all men are predators. For good and positive thoughts generally there is no concern. Many of our thoughts can limit us and cause difficulties.

When you are unaware of the hidden pattern, you will continue to be drawn to the wrong kind of person or situation who epitomises your beliefs. It must be said that in many cases, it takes a lot of work to pull away from these kinds of situations or destructive relationships. The pull to stay with what we know and what we believe we deserve is strong.

Often these situations create a feeling of being 'stuck'. You are unsure what to do, never mind how to make changes. It can feel like there is no light at the end of the tunnel. More often than not you don't understand what causes the 'stuck' feeling or why you are behaving the way you are. 'I can't seem to control it' or 'I can't help it' are common statements. The thinking is autopilot and the response follows, therefore a pattern. When we can spot our patterns, we are well on our way to shifting them, so remember anything is achievable.

Model of Love

Love is something that we naturally want although this will look different for each people. It is a normal desire to be wanted, loved and believed in. After all, we are sociable creatures. We want interaction, to engage, share, be inspired and experience life with others. Many problems around our interactions stem from the pull to being liked and wanted. How we get that from each other varies and is affected by so many components. When we understand many of these potential components, we can take a new path.

The problems start with behaviours which are displayed when people have an unhealthy need for love to feel fulfilled. When we have been shown a healthy model of love, then we are more likely to create a happy life. However, it becomes a challenge when we don't know what it is we are seeking because it hasn't been shown to us. How will we know that love has shown up, if we are not clear on what it looks like. We may even miss it when it does appear!

Each of us will show love in different ways and these differences in themselves can cause conflict. What is perceived as love by one person is a million miles for another. People can be unhappy in relationships due to expectations which have come from the completely different models of love or relationships. As we know these can come from formative years or just different personalities. Some people show love in acts of service, some in gifts or large displays of affection.

The way we demonstrate and feel love is usually closely linked to what we have witnessed. Some can show love freely and others find it more difficult. We all know people who show their affection outwardly, they wear their heart on their sleeve and appear to find it easy to be loving. As a child they have known that they are loved and there is little doubt in their mind. Alternatively, there are some where love has been less apparent. Whether this is learned from the parents relationships or from how they were treated.

A child of parents who found it hard to show love to one another could become an adult with a constant need for love, approval and reassurance. A single parent situation means a child may not have witnessed parents in a relationship. Any of these situations can play out as constantly people-pleasing, wanting to be liked or spending a lot of time fearing rejection. This can create an insecure or anxious person who will continue to believe that they won't get anything right, they are not lovable, and this will lead to some of the unhealthy behaviours we will explore. All this subsequently holding them back in the decisions they make in their lives.

We can learn this behaviour, both positive and negative and this becomes how we function as an adult. The goal though is to work very hard to have it the way we want rather than the way we were shown. Any new positive behaviours can be learned with effort, there will be a mould to break and a new path to take.

The main reason people stay broken after breakups or family feuds is that they have false beliefs about relationships stored in their subconscious. The damage caused by a previous challenge has left false beliefs like 'I will never find the right one'; 'I am not deserving'; 'it must be me'; 'people will always hurt me'; 'I can't trust anyone'; 'all men are controlling'; or 'all women are too emotional'.

These beliefs can lead to possessiveness, jealousy or other sabotaging behaviours and will affect any relationship if they are not managed carefully. Many problems arise in relationships simply because differences are not appreciated. Awareness and acceptance of them can free a couple or a family member from feeling constantly compromised. Then there can be a movement towards a common ground where both feel safe and are able to be themselves.

The good news is that we can unlearn any negative behaviours and change! When someone feels safe and understands what lies beneath the discomfort, then this kind of situation can start to change.

Limiting self-beliefs

As we have acknowledged, it is not to be underestimated how powerful self-limiting beliefs are and to know that they can rule our lives. Our subconscious mind hold onto any beliefs we have about ourselves, positive or negative, and this will determine how we behave. These beliefs are often deep-rooted and, if not explored and changed, will define you. The negative ones will limit your experiences and can stop you from pushing yourself into new, different or challenging situations, including relationships. When this becomes a way of being, you then limit your hopes and expectations. This is likely to distract you from your own true path.

When we have negative thinking patterns, then we are very likely to experience issues. It can feel overwhelming when we are constantly unhappy or unsettled and we often put this down to someone else's behaviour. By understanding why we have responded in this way is key to moving on. Our self-limiting or negative beliefs cause us to distort and interpret situations. Whatever you believe about yourself affects you in most, if not all situations. For example, if you believe you don't deserve to be treated well, then you are likely to attract people who treat you poorly and put you down. Your belief of yourself is then validated. This kind of person is clearly not a positive influence in your life, although the secret message is more about you than them. The feedback for you and the reason you attracted them into your life, was for you to see these, often hidden beliefs and work towards changing them.

Once these are realised and changed then you can attract the right things in your life. Remembering that many beliefs about yourself are not true. It can never be true that 'you don't deserve love' can it? Your beliefs and decisions are created based on what has happened to you, how people have communicated and interacted with you. This combination creates your reality, your interpretation. This interpretation will then become your truth.

Just as your mind 'protects' you by providing an automatic response to a danger or perceived danger, it is also constantly searching for any evidence that a belief is true. The mind creates an internal response to a situation based on the information that is stored. For example, a husband hasn't texted during the day to check if his wife is feeling better and this can be interpreted as he doesn't care. The mind automatically gives a thought relating to the beliefs within. It may be 'This has happened to us before, so watch out' or 'You are not good enough, so he/she isn't interested in you'. Another example would be two colleagues huddled together in the office and a third person, who has issues with self-confidence, interprets this as them talking about her and taking it personally.

When we doubt ourselves, maybe whether we are good enough or not lovable, not able to be successful in a relationship, job, or anything else for that matter, it has a direct impact on almost everything — most importantly, on our happiness. Paying attention to these negative thoughts and beliefs starts us on a journey of self-discovery. As we have discussed, when we are unaware of our own behaviour, notice we are likely to blame someone else and spot our own confusion or misery. We can lose sight of who we are, feel lost and hence be stuck in the re-sit class. How we see ourselves plays out in our life and we can only break these patterns when we admit our own part.

It is fair to say that we all have limiting beliefs in some shape or another. What we will concentrate on now is when the impact of these beliefs is destructive. Regardless of any limiting belief, as humans there is an innate, strong desire to be liked and loved. This can present itself in an unhealthy way and overrule everything else. When there are limiting self beliefs which are 'playing out', the need becomes desperate to please, to seek approval and be loved. What will follow are behaviours to try and settle these feelings of discomfort, which is often rooted in insecure or doubt based thinking. The behaviours then become a response, sometimes erratic or irrational, and certainly not one that is necessarily favourable or positive.

Watch out

Some negative beliefs can be kept buried and can be less obvious on a day-to-day basis. They can be triggered, often unexpectedly, when a new situation or person comes along. Sometimes it can come as a surprise! For example, a new relationship prompts a limiting belief relating to insecurity to pop up, maybe in response to something the new partner is doing without realising. These triggers can happen in all different settings. It may be at work. You are plodding away happily, and you get a new role or promotion. You had been fine in the old role but your new manager has a different approach. They are quite abrupt in their communication. This throws you into a place of doubt, uncertainty and can lead you to question your ability and performance. This triggers an emotional response based on an old memory and so unlocks your limiting self-beliefs.

In a personal situation, you might constantly refuse invitations to functions, events or even dates because of the belief that no one enjoys your company or is interested in anything you have to say - after all, you may believe that you don't have anything interesting to say! Or you may make yourself go to a party and when you get there you feel awkward, on the edge of the conversations and not engaged, which reinforces your beliefs that you are not popular. You start to feel isolated by everyone else but, in fact, you have isolated yourself and there lies the problem. In many situations, we find ourselves thinking that others are judging us and a feeling of inferiority grows. Through your limiting beliefs, you may have put others in a superior position, although it is you that is feeling inferior.

If this is you, in any varying degree, and this kind of situation sounds familiar, it is a huge step to acknowledge this. Well done! As we venture through this journey together, we will be looking at what you can do with this new awareness and how you can make positive changes.

Saboteurs

In many instances, our thoughts and responses are positive so we make decisions, take action and keep safe, although we all have times when this is not the case.

Let's now look at how your limiting beliefs affect your responses and behaviours. You might describe it like a voice in your head which acts like a saboteur, a negative voice holding you back. These saboteurs are lurking in the mind and will pop up at any time. It is that voice in your head that is pulling you up, constantly saying things like 'You could never do that', 'They won't like you', 'It is too good to be true and it won't last' or 'I never get this lucky'. This thinking will and does stop you in your tracks and affects your actions and decisions.

The internal voice can be like a constant chatter in your mind. It is always on your case telling you what you can and can't do. It is switched on without your permission. It's like a 'goodie' and a 'baddie' on each shoulder having an argument, triggering emotions and affecting your behaviours. This constant chit chat can be exhausting and the baddie voice is, more often than not, the loudest. These are your limiting beliefs at large and it can be these that change your decisions and probably your life course.

Imagine being with a group of friends you have known for years. A few in the group are talking about when they went to the cinema but you knew nothing about it. A negative belief lurking inside is triggered instantly leading you to feel left out. Why didn't they include you? There could be a rational reason why this event took place and yet your mind has taken over with no room for logic! You are quiet, not engaging in the rest of the occasion, and more than likely will go home dwelling over the situation. This scenario has probably stirred up some deep-rooted, unresolved beliefs that you are not liked, which you have made true because you are struggling to like yourself.

These saboteurs are closely connected to beliefs deep within your psyche. Self-sabotage leads to negative and damaging behaviour, such as acting as if you don't deserve to be happy, making comments which put yourself down or limit your experiences. It can play out by you constantly taking everything personally or shy away from being assertive in a situation. There is a likelihood that you assume that the other person is deliberately hurting you, and then there is a risk that you are likely to blame them.

When you take a moment to notice your own internal voice and chatter, then your awareness changes and you can start to challenge your own thinking. What kind of chatter do you notice when you are feeling insecure, anxious or rejected? Do you hear 'It must be me', 'You don't deserve happiness anyway', or 'Is it all my fault?' When you are listening to your self-saboteurs you become so worried and afraid of what might happen that you become frozen in your fears. It can develop into mistrust, worry, anxiety, hopelessness and powerlessness. It can paralyse you and affect your progress in life. It can also be a fleeting moment in time when you feel unable to move forward with something small and trivial.

A quick reframe

Let's look at changing some negative thoughts about yourself. Imagine this scenario: would you let a burglar come into your home, eat all your food, use all your things and squat there? I am pretty sure the answer would be a big NO, so why would you allow negative, unwanted thoughts, either about yourself or others, to dominate your mind?

These 'rent-free lodgers' are more than likely distracting you and preventing you from getting on with your day - or even your life. For example, you might be stressing about what you said to someone, running the story over and over again in your mind and driving yourself to distraction. Or you might be thinking that someone in your life is unhappy being with you because they don't tell you they love you regularly.

You spend hours trying to work out what you have done or how you can change it. But change what; as the reality isn't as you imagine it. These scenarios are in everyday life and we can easily get lost in so much detail and allow others to be rent free in our head. It is common for us to get upset, particularly with others, when we spend time worrying about something that is actually out of our control. It is quite interesting to notice that we are often focused on the parts we can't control as a distraction to not doing what actually is need, which is in our control. And this ultimately leads to drama which we will look at shortly.

Let's stop and take a look at this yourself with this next exercise:

STEP to CHANGE

Your self-talk

Your self-talk

Take a moment to think about your own situation.

Take some time to notice what thoughts are in your mind NOW...

These maybe about yourself, others or a situation. See if you can separate them under these headings.

In my control

Positive thoughts

Out of my control

Negative thoughts

Some negative thoughts and beliefs that some people have:

- 'I am angry with my boyfriend'.
- 'I can't do the presentation for work'.
- 'When will it all stop?'
- 'Bad things always happen to me'.
- 'I am useless'.
- 'Everything would be ok, if she did things differently'.
- 'Why do people let me down?'
- 'If it wasn't for my parents things would be ok'.
- 'I don't deserve to have love'.
- 'It's all my fault'.
- 'I messed up'.

Self-fulfilling prophecy

You construct your own reality. When you expect things to happen to you or go a certain way based on your internal world, this is described as a self-fulfilling prophecy. This expectation, positive or negative, affects your behaviour and subsequently the outcome. You have caused something to happen by believing or simply thinking it will come true. If you repeat 'I can, I can' as you run up a hill, you will probably make it. However, if you tell yourself you won't make it, you will run out of steam.

Your own beliefs play a big part in this process as they affect the reality. When you have taken the time to notice your limiting thoughts, you will start to see their power and how much these affect you and your life. The first and vital step to making changes is being aware of these thoughts, beliefs and limits within you. It is from this position that you can challenge yourself and this thinking. Hearing your own thoughts about yourself and your life, you can start to make sense of why situations go the way they do and what part you play in this.

The following case study illustrates the point:

CASE STUDY

Wendy and her boyfriend, Peter, had been invited to a party for one of Wendy's friends. Wendy was a social butterfly but Peter struggled with meeting new people and was nervous beforehand. He was already worrying about not knowing anyone, whether anyone would talk to him or if he would feel awkward. He walked in with all these thoughts and worries so he didn't feel relaxed and was projecting these negative emotions, despite trying hard not to.

She, on the other hand, was happy catching up, chatting and thoroughly enjoying herself. As the evening wore on, Peter was feeling increasingly uncomfortable, anxious and isolated. He did nothing to alleviate these feelings because, although he knew a few people, he was getting so annoyed with Wendy that he could hardly speak to them. He was angry with her for leaving him so much on his own and making him 'look a fool'. Of course, the reality was that no one else was thinking that; it was his own internal world that was confusing the situation with his own mental and emotional patterns.

Peter searched for Wendy and gave her a barrage of angry words, accusing her of leaving him, saying she was being so selfish. Yet, in reality, what had actually occurred here? In her world, his friends were there too and they were both spending time with their respective friends. Peter's lens of the situation was completely different to Wendy's.

Worry thinking

Everyone is different. We all have a unique set of expectations and beliefs and that is why two people can react completely differently in the same situation. A single situation might trigger worry in one person and not in another. Worry thinkers tend to take a negative view. It is a bit like the chicken and egg debate, which came first? The worry that makes people think negatively or the thinking negatively that makes people worry?

As we have said, if we always worry about bad outcomes then the future will always look bleak. Similarly, if you feel down, then small problems will probably seem larger than they really are.

With your own list of negative, unhelpful, blaming, repetitive or damaging thoughts from the previous exercise, the question to ask is, 'Why do I allow all this negative stuff to go round and round in my head? What is its purpose?' It is something we are all guilty of and, weirdly, we seem to spend more time re-running the things that don't work out rather than reliving the good times!

Another question to ask yourself is do you notice if this 'worry thinking' actually serves any purpose or creates a positive outcome? It definitely doesn't; the situation is still the same! Worrying about something doesn't change anything about the situation and it certainly has no purpose when we worry about other people's actions. Reflective thinking only works when we are focused on something that we can control or when we are able to consider alternatives for ourselves.

Once you start to identify your own thinking and how your 'stuff' plays out, then you can start to make sense of your interactions with yourself and others. People will not always do what you want or need them to do. Being able to identify your own triggers gives you a chance to notice how you respond to others and how they respond to you. This allows you to become more flexible and start to change the outcome.

Getting into drama

Within families, relationships and friendships we all have roles with each other and it's like we are characters in the story. There is so much value in getting honest with ourselves and checking whether your character is a healthy one. Often, we are running an old story with unhelpful beliefs and this then causes drama. This becomes a blockage within the relationship.

What do we mean when we 'get into drama'. Generally people get into drama when things are not going the way they want them too or when an unexpected situation pops up. This can trigger the instant, internal emotional responses we have explored. Much of our negative thinking or our internal interpretations can lead us to be 'in drama' with ourselves, others or a situation. More often than not we are already in drama before we have even realised it. Being aware helps us to respond differently.

A model to help us understand the roles we take and how we all behave when we feel we are not getting our own way or feeling unsettled is called the Karpman's Drama Triangle.

In the model, there are three positions: the Persecutor, the Victim and the Rescuer. Each position can be adopted to try and manipulate the situation or gain control. These positions tell us a lot about each person and can show up self-limiting beliefs and issues around self respect.

We can have a tendency to adopt one of these roles, such as seeing everything to have a negative impact on you (the victim), or always being angry with the world and blaming everyone else for your misfortune (the persecutor). The Rescuer would find themselves trying to fix everyone else, paying little attention to themselves and often keeping people in the victim position or allowing the persecutor to stay in their position. It is also possible and common to move between the positions, driven by the situation or a person. This can literally happen within one challenging conversation. Analysing these roles helps to make sense of some unhealthy behaviour which ultimately results in a negative outcome.

These roles can be learned from others. We can sometimes mirror other influential people in our lives. For example, a child may witness a mother say that she has always struggled through life and no one has helped her or a father's behaviours are aggressive or controlling. The child may believe this is how to behave.

A symptom of being in drama is to look to blame someone or something else, particularly during a disagreement. The argument leads both parties to swap positions, both trying to get their view point heard. There is a drive to look for evidence that proves their point and ignore any evidence that contradicts it.

All parties are unlikely to take any personal responsibility and will have their 'heels dug in' or feel stuck. People can often move from one position to another very quickly. When anyone is in drama, because of their irrational thinking and floods of hormones, they are likely to make poor decisions, say something they may regret and be acting based on their interpretation of the situation. Each person is likely to be defending their corner, coming from a position of vulnerability, responding from a place of stress or a negative emotional state. It is probable that they are not being rational and blaming the other person. The interactions won't be particularly healthy, and conversations become distorted and misunderstanding is rife.

We can find ourselves in drama at the flick of a switch. It can be something as simple as someone has forgotten to put the bins out and the other person is furious. Alternatively, the drama can play right through a relationship, where insecurities are challenging each person to feel like a victim or a perpetrator and each is blaming the other for their upset, like Peter and Wendy from earlier.

The roles

Let's now look in more detail at the characteristics for each of these in turn. As you read them, keep in mind which roles or parts of the role resonate with you and also who in your life behaves in this way.

Victim role – 'Why does this keep happening to me?'

A victim is someone who usually feels overwhelmed by their own sense of vulnerability, inadequacy or powerlessness. They do not take responsibility for themselves or safeguard their own power.

Whether we know, admit it, or not, most of us react to life as victims. There are a lot of influences which force people to think that they are at the effect of something. It clearly doesn't work although we can all be caught in it. We often feel badly done by or we believe there a lot of things that are done to us. Victim thinking can prevent us from taking responsibility for ourselves. Life is unfair and things keep happening to us. Victims tend to believe that they are powerless to make any changes and they are not worthy, not good enough or weaker than another person. This creates feelings of hurt, fear, and a sense of being stuck. As a result, victims often find themselves either people-pleasing, blaming or punishing themselves, having lower self-esteem, being needy or believing people are superior or better than them. All these behaviours are coming from a place of fear and become a way to gain some relief. 'Either feel sorry for me, or I will feel sorry for myself'.

Within families, relationships, friendships or at work we can adopt any position. We can put ourselves into the positions or be pulled in by another. Because of another person's actions, a victim can take the stance that 'Things never work out for me', and 'It is all my fault'. From this position, there is a tendency to interpret a lot of what others say as a criticism or to take comments personally. In some situations, a victim can feel so low about themselves that they often see others as more powerful and controlling.

A victim can build resentment, which can manifest itself into retaliation and then the positions can rotate. The victim then becomes a perpetrator, blaming the other person. All thoughts and behaviours from these positions are negative towards others in the drama.

Being a victim can become part of our identity and, even though destructive, it is a strange sort of comfort zone. It becomes familiar and, in some instances, we only know ourselves with these negative beliefs and thoughts. A relationship can then be formed with a perpetrator who treats us as we believe we deserve. Sometimes we internalise the feelings, which eats away at us. Ultimately, we get stuck and don't have the life we want. 'Why does this keep happening to me'?

This thinking can keep us stuck in the re-sit class unless we are open and acknowledge our own responsibility.

For a victim to feel better, they may seek out a rescuer to take care of them. Someone who will listen to our stories and feel sorry for us. The rescuer, though well meaning, is likely to offer their advice which to the victim can feel overwhelming. The victim could move to the persecutor position and persecute their rescuer. Victim will always feel like a victim until they take responsibility for themselves.

Persecutor role – 'it's their fault'

The persecutor believes that other people are to blame and that they need to change to make things better.

Persecutors can seek out a victim to blame and are unaware of their blaming tactics. They feel that attack is warranted and necessary for self-protection as they usually believe that their way is the only way. They subsequently think or say things like 'she is useless', 'he does it deliberately', 'you're doing it all wrong', or 'you should have known better'. They can easily justify their vengeful behaviour - 'they asked for it, they got what they deserve', or 'it was their fault anyway'. Even though their actions are usually somewhat aggressive, they often feel that the world is dangerous and people can't be trusted so they think 'I need to get them before they hurt me'. Persecutors can present more passively too, it isn't always an aggressive approach.

The position of persecutor is synonymous with being unaware of one's own power and therefore discounting it. Either way the power used is negative and often destructive. Any person within the triangle may at any time switch roles. However their own internal perception may be that they are being persecuted, and that they are the victim. There are of course instances in which the persecutor is knowingly and maliciously persecuting the other person.

Persecutors can spend their lives in a tense, perpetual cringe against the next blow or the next crisis, sure that there's always a missile of bad luck lurking with their name on it, about to hit its mark. Like a victim, they can take comments personally or interpret them as a criticism. They can genuinely believe that the other people are wrong and they blame them for difficulties. The behaviours, which fit well with this position, can include being right, being negative, being critical or judgemental. All because they are not prepared to look at themselves and see their part in the situation.

While we all have a set of principles within us and a strong sense of what is right and wrong, persecutors can portray this quite forcefully. They often place a strong set of principles on themselves and others. They begin to judge other's actions and get annoyed because they are not meeting their standards. The response can be expressed as anger, jealousy or self pity – 'How could they have done that to me'? As with any of the positions of the drama triangle, there is a risk that situations will be interpreted incorrectly, and it is these interpretations that cause the most conflict. There is blame and very little reflection on what is actually causing the problem.

Rescuer role - 'I'll save you'

The position that is less obvious is that of the rescuer and yet this can be just as unhealthy as the others. They are likely to believe they must help others and will look to help a specific person or type of person. Their approach to helping and supporting can be disempowering and training people to take up or be held in the victim role.

A rescuer is someone who often does not own their own vulnerability and seeks instead to "rescue" those whom they see as vulnerable. The traits of a rescuer are that they often do or believe they do more than

50% of the work, they may offer help unasked, rather than find out if and how the other person wants to be supported. What the rescuer agrees to do may, in actual fact, not be what they really want to do. This means that the rescuer may then often end up feeling hard done by or resentful, used or unappreciated in some way.

The rescuer does not take responsibility for themselves, but rather likes to take responsibility for the perceived victim. The rescuer usually ends up feeling like the victim, but sometimes may be perceived by others, who are on the outside looking in, as being the persecutor because they can be quite bossy or demanding.

The rescuer can smother, control and manipulate others, believing 'It's for their own good'. They want to 'fix' the victim and gain personal achievement by feeling valued and worthwhile. Their behaviours can pacify the persecutor and then build up resentment towards them. The huge risk for the rescuer is they are likely to burn out because what they are doing is not sustainable. An inevitable outcome is to eventually take the position of the victim - 'No matter how much I do, it's never enough'.

Just to clarify, the rescuer position is different from someone who is supporting or offering wanted guidance. We can be a helpful friend as long as the other person has asked for help or advice!

Even then, your advice may not be right for the other person. It may be good advice but the victim may not be ready or doesn't want to hear it (some people stay in victim mode and are unable to take action for themselves). We all need to want to take responsibility for ourselves rather than be 'fixed' by someone else which can feel disempowering.

In some dynamics, a person is permanently in the rescuer position within a family, a relationship or a group. They are expected to do everything, come up with all the solutions and generally be there for everyone else. When we see this in younger years, a behaviour pattern can form where the rescuer is so busy looking out for everyone else that they are then unsure of who they are themselves and certainty won't be getting what is actually right for them.

Being aware of the positions on the drama triangle helps to step back, think and respond differently.

STEP to CHANGE

You in DRAMA

You in DRAMA

Take a moment to think about your own situation.

Can you identify yourself in any of the drama roles? Do these roles define you?

PERSECUTOR (Blaming others):...

VICTIM (Blame self): ....

RESCUER (Fixing others): ....

.... With WHO?

.... With WHO?

.... With WHO?

Each of the positions are taken up as a result of an issue being discounted or disowned. To remedy this the:

Rescuer needs to take responsibility for him/herself, connect with their power and acknowledge their vulnerability.

Victim needs to own their vulnerability, take responsibility for themselves and recognise that they have power and are able to use it appropriately.

Persecutor needs initially to own their power, not use it covertly and not be afraid of it.

All positions have choices and getting out of drama helps to see them.

Your thoughts

More often than not if we are in drama, either position, we are unlikely to be aware of our thoughts. As you become more aware of your thinking and your behaviours - and that of others - it is useful to notice what kind of thoughts consume your mind and how much these impact on you.

Remembering we can't stop thoughts and many thoughts appear to happen automatically. We don't take the time to reflect on them or on our instant responses. If your thoughts are full of blame or emotions then you are unlikely to make a clear, rational decision. Another indicator that you are in drama. In her book, Eat, Pray, Love author Elizabeth Gilbert said, "we need to learn to select our thoughts as we do our clothes".

Drama behaviours

We will now spend some time looking at different resulting behaviours when we find ourselves in drama. By acknowledging these behaviours, we can make changes.

Comparing ourselves to others

Jealousy can come from comparing ourselves to others. It can play a big part of people's relationships and these are closely linked to the limiting beliefs we have explored. Just to start, let's just have a quick look at the difference between jealousy and envy. The English dictionary explains that we feel jealous of a person but envious of belongings and things. They are certainly not the same e.g. I am jealous of my girlfriend when she talks to someone versus I am envious he drives a Porsche. Either can feed the need to compare to others and create unhelpful feelings towards the other person and then limiting thoughts about ourselves.

An inevitable impact of being in a victim position is that we judge ourselves against other people and usually in a negative way. When we are being irrational and in drama we can lose perspective. We see everything as a threat or we feel inadequate. The result is irrational thinking and even a meltdown.

There are definite advantages and disadvantages to comparing to others. It can be positive because it can drive and motivate us. However, we do need to remember that we are all different, and what works for one person does not necessarily mean that it would be right for another. When comparing is positive, others can be a catalyst to making changes or improvements in our lives. Observing other people can be beneficial because, like window shopping, it helps us identify what we like or dislike. Some people will teach us simply by showing us how we don't want to be!

Comparing is problematic when we see ourselves in a negative light or inferior to others. This can get quite out of control and is destructive. Issues arise when we draw conclusions about the quality of other people's lives based purely on what we see - social media is a perfect example. We never really know what's happening in other people's lives, so we should never make assumptions, especially when this has a negative impact on us. When we are comparing ourselves, there is a chance that any limiting beliefs can pop up again, which can distort our thinking and leave us feeling threatened or inferior. As we now know, it is our mind that is creating these false ideas

Is your glass half full or half empty?

Life events and challenging times will naturally cause people to feel upset and sometimes to be bitter about the world. Losing a parent, divorce or an illness will leave a person downbeat. The problem arises when the negativity and unhappiness take over and become a permanent habit for someone. They often or even always seem to be complaining, ready and eager to find fault - even in the people they love the most, or themselves! There is always a negative story to report, with some almost enjoying being the bearer of bad news.

For some people, it is as if they have negativity running through their veins and they appear to be gleeful being negative, even though this is often not in their awareness. They are more likely to focus on the imperfection in situations and talk about things they dislike. They have a cynical, pessimistic attitude, which can present as being moody or grumpy, never happy or they have more of a subtle prickly, sarcastic edge to them. Many don't even know they are doing it and find it difficult to get out of this mindset. It is not necessarily on purpose; it is just their way. However, we know that negativity is draining. Being aware that this is the case is the first port of call. Then we can look for an alternative approach.

An easy way to look at this is through the metaphor: glass half full or half empty? It explains so much about how different people are. Some people will naturally see life full of opportunities, can see the positive and they perceive their life as full of good things. They tend to be optimistic and forward thinking people.

Some people are more likely to think the opposite, that the glass is half empty. They are more likely to see the negative first, be more pessimistic and always wonder what could go wrong. They can focus on what they don't have in their life and think 'what if....'. This type of thinking holds people back although does act as a coping mechanism.

Negativity hinders people in two ways. Firstly, it is unpleasant to be around someone who is projecting negative vibes. When we are either being that negative person or have negative people around us, we are bound to be unhappy in this wearing environment. Secondly, negative people are usually holding themselves back because they see the worst in everything. They struggle to connect with people because they keep finding flaws or are too critical about their own efforts to move forward. They can see themselves as victims of life.

A symptom of negativity is constant complaining regardless of the topic or argument. Negative people can be finely tuned to notice the flaws in activities, things, others or, of course, in themselves! They will be the one that 'has' to point something out in any situation or 'has' to negate a positive remark with the word 'but'. They will voice why something won't work or why it's a bad idea, often without a rational explanation and often resulting in others feeling hurt and disheartened. Remember, this kind of behaviour can be learned from observing parents and others. People displaying this behaviour will be very difficult to be around for more positive, glass half full people as it will feel like their bubble is constantly being burst or that the other person doesn't approve.

Interestingly, often at the heart of negativity is a lack of self-love. It is often driven by a fear of being disrespected by others, of not being loved, or a fear that bad things are going to happen. When a person makes negative comments, they may be using this to feel better about themselves (a type of limiting belief), whether to knock everything down to their level or to boost their own ego by feeling smart and capable by noticing the flaws. The defence mechanism is to be negative, risk averse and often mistrusting. For some, their past experiences have created a belief that the world is a disappointing and negative place.

It is very common to have internal negative thinking and negative self-talk. This is different to people who talk negatively about and towards others. Self-talk is often a dominant trait in those in the victim role. It is an internal negative voice on repeat: 'Why can't I change', 'I'll never get what I want', 'This is pointless', or ' I always mess up'. These thoughts are directly linked to sadness, anxiety, lethargy, lack of motivation and self-doubt. The negative internal chatter then clouds the judgement of a situation, a person or ourselves which can come from deep within. 'It must be me' is a typical response, taking or giving the blame yet, actually, taking no responsibility.

The constant critic

We all have an opinion on things, but there are some who think that it is their given right to express their opinion, even when it is not really helpful. This can come in many forms and, depending on the delivery or the listener, can be interpreted as a criticism. It can come across as 'You are not doing what I would like you to do', so I will comment and criticise you until you see things my way! This is not necessarily done maliciously, and their heart is often in the right place, but because of the way it is said it can easily be interpreted as negative.

When we know that some people are just like this, we can stop seeing it as a personal attack and then manage the situation and ourselves better. They may be like this as a result of experiences from younger years, limiting beliefs, to feel powerful or quite simply a bad habit, a habit which makes it impossible to not comment or find fault in others.

Remember that many of these behaviours are not done consciously; they are a default position of a persecutor.

Sometimes people make competitive comments which are not necessarily criticism, although could be heard as such. For example a parent is struggling with two small children and her mother says, 'Imagine what it was like having four, you have it easy'. This can be perceived as unsupportive and taken personally. She is acknowledging how challenging it is having small children, although this could even be interpreted as 'You know nothing' or 'It's a shame that you're not perfect'.

These scenarios are neither productive nor pleasant and cause challenges and conflict. The victim will feel attacked, undermined and will probably defend their corner. This kind of behaviour can happen in any situations in life: in partnerships, with parents, friends and colleagues or the boss. It is usually the closer the relationship, the more painful the impact, although all cases are different.

Let's have a look at where you are now with this next exercise.

STEP to CHANGE

Where are you?

Where are you?

Take a moment to think about your situation.

Let's stop and see where you are.

Would you describe yourself as:

Glass half FULL   or   Glass half EMPTY

How do you respond to new things?

POSITIVELY, give it a go   or   CAUTIOUSLY, what if... Can't

How do you view the world around you?

Do you see POSSIBILITIES   or   OBSTACLES

How do you frame your expectations?

Are you OPTIMISTIC   or   PESSIMISTIC

Regardless of whether you glass is half full or half empty, there is always room to top it up.

Expecting the worst

Another habit people can be in is always expecting the worst. For some this can feel like a safety mechanism. It allows them to be forewarned and forearmed against any eventuality. While it can be positive to be organised and prepared, for some there can be a tendency to dread going somewhere new or doing something for the first time thinking - 'it is going to be terrible'. The anxiety and fear can, in some cases, escalate beyond anything tangible and while the fight or flight response is natural, it is often unwarranted due to this fear-based thinking. This can result in periods of acute anxiety and in some cases a constant flux.

This tendency to be unduly concerned in a situation can be overwhelming, potentially sending yourself and other people into panic or frustration and making the situation even more difficult. For example, your flight is cancelled and you go straight to panic about how you are going to get there and what will happen to you. When you are in this kind of thinking, your solution-thinking mind has been switched off and the situations feel more difficult to manage.

This type of pessimistic thinking can create problems in other relationships and may be linked to those self-limiting beliefs. For example, you are expecting a romantic evening with your partner and you receive a text to say that they are running late. In your mind, this is an instant disaster. You hit your sabotage button, the internal chatter is switched on automatically - 'This is all ruined now'. You instantly think that they don't want to see you, they are not feeling the same way as you do about them, they don't prioritise the relationship, or you as much as you do, and even, in the extreme, this must be the end of the relationship.

By the time your partner arrives, you are furious or upset so much so that the evening is ruined. It doesn't matter whatever gets said or done, your emotions are roaring and your reactions are disproportionate. The irrational has taken over the rational and you are either being a victim or a perpetrator, or a mix of both. Whichever, the internal belief system has ruled the situation and there has been no room for thinking straight about other possibilities.

Fear of disappointment

The fear of being a disappointment to someone, quite commonly your parents or a partner, or interpreting that you are a failure is also often visible when you are in a victim role. By living in fear of disappointing others or getting it wrong, you are likely to make decisions that are not right for you in an attempt to please others.

For many of us, seeking approval is inherent. This starts as a child seeking to gain parental approval. You probably tried your best and as you were learning and developing you invariably made mistakes. It may have been that you didn't have a solid benchmark or a good role model. You may have been expected to do things that your own parents didn't do very well themselves. For example, maybe you were encouraged to make new friends at a club and yet your parents are not particularly confident in social settings themselves. This can cause a lot of confusion in a young mind.

In many instances, it may go like this - what the child got wrong was picked up on and there was little praise or recognition for what was done well. The parent's intention may have been to motivate the child to try harder and improve, although the child was left feeling like they couldn't make mum and/or dad happy. The pattern is then brought into adult life and the need to seek approval or positive attention becomes so important it ends up being destructive. We can put ourselves in difficult and even vulnerable situations seeking this attention and love.

A common reaction is that people overcompensate to gain approval, which then becomes the norm. For example, someone puts themselves at another's beck and call; whatever they ask for or whenever they make contact, the other person is available. This is not sustainable or healthy and prevents someone from living their own life. It can also lead to resentment and unhappiness and there is a risk that they will not be being true to themselves. By not putting yourself first you can find yourself miles away from being yourself and not travelling on your own true path.

Self-punishment

When we feel down on ourselves, taking other people's actions and comments personally and feeling like life is not going the way we want, we can be very hard on ourselves. Our self-talk will be damning and can cause a lot of upset. People self-punish in many ways, such as becoming isolated because they feel so bad, yelling at themselves, neglecting their physical needs and, in some instances, feeling compelled to inflict physical harm on themselves (examples of self-punishment include using alcohol and other substances, promiscuity, eating disorders, self-harm and gambling). They convince themselves that 'it's my fault' or they use physical pain to distract them from the emotional pain.

Self-punishment can be persistent and it can also act as self-defence against the pain of life. We can turn against ourselves in anger when we feel a lack of control, a failure, rejected or even mildly embarrassed.

We all have a strong desire for connection, acceptance, success and approval, but we need to face the reality that people can reject us, be disappointed with us and put their needs above ours. If you feel repeatedly shot down, ignored, scorned, abused or attacked, then self-punishment can be a by-product.

Let's look at an example where self-punishment can creep in:

CASE STUDY

Janet was unhappy, had a poor view of herself and thought that she constantly made bad decisions. Her self-talk was I am so useless, I am lazy, what must people think of me? and she felt trapped. She questioned everything she did and found herself going over and over her actions and conversations with no positive outcome. Over time this impacted on her self-esteem, her self-worth and her energy. She had no capacity to cope and when she felt stressed she would reach automatically for food, particularly chocolate and biscuits. She would then beat herself up after she had binged and knew that she had jeopardised any weight loss. She felt guilty and used to think, What's the point? I am a failure! and so the cycle of self-punishment continued.

While this was happening, she was trying to diet and was constantly unhappy with herself and her eating habits. She had tried every diet going and her weight was rarely under control. When she was able to move her focus from the food and onto how she felt about herself, she had an opportunity to make changes. She realised her negative beliefs about herself were holding her back, which was pushing her to eat the wrong kind of foods. When she started to believe in herself, she became focused on herself and her health, and started to make healthy choices. This had a direct impact on her body image and therefore increased her confidence and self-worth.

A common reason why change can feel impossible is because old, repetitive patterns playing out are familiar to us. They are ingrained. When we slip up, these old habits are usually stronger than the new desired state. It is like a safety blanket; for Janet, the safety blanket became her eating. There is a tendency to beat ourselves up when we have slipped up rather than paying attention to what happened and recommitting to try again. Let's now think of any failure or setback as valuable feedback! Being aware of our thinking and habits is vital before jumping to judgement. The outcome can be completely different.

"There is no failure just feedback."

For some, self-punishment can reduce feelings of discomfort. Unresolved issues often prevent us from enjoying life and thriving emotionally. By being hard on ourselves, thinking negatively and self-punishing, we start to ease our feelings of discomfort and free our conscience. While it feels like it is relieving our internal feelings, it has a negative impact on us and on the way others perceive us. It demonstrates to others that we are prepared to harm ourselves because we believe we have done wrong or are not good enough.

All of these negative thinking patterns have a detrimental effect on self-esteem, self-respect, self-worth and confidence. These negative feelings are damaging and draining and can leave a constant feeling of exhaustion and unhappiness. Most importantly, they often lead to poor self-care or not following the right path.

Self-blame

Both self-punishment and self-blame are closely linked to how we view ourselves and any negative limiting beliefs. When we don't believe in ourselves or live with the belief that no one values us, then we can either get into a habit of taking all or part of the blame for everything or giving ourselves a hard time when things don't work out well.

When we see ourselves in a negative light, it is an indicator that we lack self-belief and then the action of self-blame and sometimes guilt can be extremely overwhelming. There can be a lot of time and energy spent thinking and assuming that we have done something wrong, which is quite often not the case.

Let's just look at a very simple example which helps make sense of the automatic response that can happen to us all:

A couple walking down the road spot their neighbour walking towards them. The woman says to her husband, "Oh look, there's Peter from next door." She raises her arm to wave. At that instant, Peter steps closer to the curb, checks for oncoming cars and makes his way to the other side of the street. Her arm is left hanging in a half wave and the smile falls from her face. She turns to her husband and says, "What have we done wrong? I bet he's irritated because we left our bins out overnight last Thursday. He's not speaking to us."

Her husband replies "Don't be silly. He's in a hurry and didn't even see us." She is in a place of low self-esteem, ready to blame herself for the neighbour's actions and could easily cause an issue within the relationship.

Her husband is more likely in a place of high self-esteem, seeing the same scenario as an innocent occurrence, no one to blame, nothing unusual, his day and his relationship with Peter unaffected.

These patterns of thinking are then formed, and we can be quick to put ourselves down on a daily basis - 'I was so silly','I was so naive', 'how could this happen again'? The reality is we are putting our attention on the negativity and judging ourselves unfairly. Even when we accidentally drop our phone or stub our toe, what words do we utter to ourselves? Often not words of kindness but words of self-criticism - You idiot! It is important to remember that our subconscious mind is always listening to everything we say about ourselves, even simple things like this, and it takes everything to be true. It believes everything we say and the inner voice.

Albert Einstein defined insanity as "doing the same thing over and over again and expecting different results". When we know we want things to be different, we need to take action.

People-pleaser

A person who has become a 'people-pleaser' is putting other people before themselves. Just to be clear, this is different from helping each other out. When we are a helpful family member, friend or colleague, the help given has been requested, we had the capacity and energy to give it and there is an even split between helping each other.

Problems arise when we are running around after someone else too much, or not being assertive about our own needs. There is a huge risk that we are then not being true to ourselves and for some the need to please outweighs anything else. People-pleasers at their worst can cause low self-esteem and frustration. They can become indecisive and certainly make choices hoping to keep others happy. If they are asked 'What would you like to see at the cinema?' or 'Where would you like to go on holiday?' their blanket answer is likely to be 'I don't mind. What do you want to do?' People pleasers find it hard to decide for themselves as the other person's needs or demands would automatically come first. They may also be fearful of voicing an opinion, in case it might be wrong and the outcome may be disapproval, rejection or being ridiculed. This can become a habit, even a way of life and then an expectation on both parts.

Another focus for a people pleaser is they feel the need to try and prove themselves to others. There can be a tendency to become too flexible and completely submissive to others' requests. In order to make others happy, the people pleaser will do or say anything to be liked and accepted. There can also be a habit of mind reading and spending a lot of time and energy trying to think what the other person wants and needs. This is often misjudged and not actually what is needed.

When we are desperately trying to please others, we are rarely pleasing ourselves. There is a belief that if they are liked, then all will be ok. As we have said it becomes a habit and an unhealthy reliance on feedback from others.

The unconscious conflict comes because deep down we have our own hopes and dreams. These are locked into the subconscious mind and we will feel disappointed as we are not aligned to our true desires. Instead we feel as if we are being forced to do something although we are actually doing it to ourselves. This results in a lack of fulfilment and satisfaction, which subsequently can build up as resentment. The impact can be that people don't know who they are at worse, they have no idea of their purpose and life direction.

" If we fuel our journey on the opinions of others, we will run out of petrol... "

Another common behaviour is when people try to change to be with someone else or to fit in. Take Danny and Sandy from 'Grease'. Each thought that they needed to change their style and outlook to get the attention of the other and yet that wasn't the case at all. We can find ourselves trying to change our behaviour, values, looks, and even personality if we believe it means pleasing the other person or being liked. When we believe that doing whatever the other person wants will keep them happy, problems are ahead. When we make unrealistic sacrifices then it is likely to lead to unhappiness and unfulfillment.

It can be like a vicious circle; we need to feel loved, we adapt ourselves to try and make the person like us and we become unfulfilled. Then we start all over again. By not putting yourself first you can find yourself miles away from being yourself and not travelling on your own true path.

To be successful and happy, the goal is to challenge the negative thinking, to work out who you really are and then be that person, rather than someone who is driven by their negative fears. When you are able to be yourself, you will get much nearer to achieving personal fulfilment and joy.

Saying no

When we are putting others first and not taking charge of our own lives, sometimes there will be a challenge in saying 'no'. It is a tiny yet hard word for some and yet the first answer for others. When we go through life saying 'yes' constantly to please others, we will become exhausted and unhappy. This is not sustainable and is often a sign of a lack of boundaries within the relationship. The other person learns to expect you to jump for them and (as we have discussed earlier) this leads to dissatisfaction and upset. It takes great courage to be honest, say 'no' or 'not right now' and be able to speak your truth.

Seeking approval and permission

As we have said, it is quite natural as humans to seek approval and love. We are all looking for reassurance and recognition. Some have a greater need for approval and permission which in itself causes an issue. It usually means there is an internal doubt.

'Neediness' can stem from feeling a lack (or the wrong kind) of attention, particularly as a child. Maybe growing up where a sibling appeared to have more of the attention, resulting in feeling invisible. The wounds can trigger a desire to cling onto whoever comes into your life. Falling in love can activate these old feelings and some of these behaviours will then play out.

Those who were brought up with more approval and encouragement are inclined to be able to self-soothe and internally check that they are ok. Subsequently, they tend to seek less external reassurance or feedback. They tend to know they are doing ok and are less likely to need anyone else to tell them. Many know within themselves that they are doing well, although still like to hear some reassurance and feedback from someone else. Nothing wrong with that! However, it is often those who haven't had a sense of approval as children who are still looking for it as adults. This behaviour can be all-consuming, with doubts becoming dominant and a need for constant external reassurance.

Commonly someone who constantly seeks approval can also find themselves overcompensating or doing more so they will be accepted - such as people-pleasing. 'I just want to be liked' is often at the root of this type of behaviour. They continually change their behaviour to what they think other people will like and consequently this can be interpreted as being needy. Seeking approval can become like a drug; it is addictive and when out of control is tiring to keep up.

Asking for some feedback or other people's opinions is part of normal life. It is important though that this doesn't dominate personal decisions.

" Many people spend years looking outside for the answer rather than inside... "

Let's face it, we all like to hear some positive encouragement and feedback but this needs to be coupled with some from ourselves.

It is important to be able to acknowledge our own achievements rather than always looking to someone else. It's important to be able to speak up confidently for ourselves, trust our own mind and ultimately look out for number one, which is you.

When we have a need for approval, we often value the opinion and needs of someone else above our own. Although it is quite common for our decision-making process to be considerate of others, we can sometimes sacrifice our own hopes and dreams in order to have the approval of others.

To gain this kind of reassurance, a common behaviour would be the need to talk about every little detail of what is happening in a relationship. There is a constant desire to know how the other person is feeling, what they are thinking and often a desperation for an immediate response. An example of this could be a multitude of missed calls, when apart, as the need for reassurance builds up. This frantic need acts as a mechanism to settle fears or doubts and can create intense relationships. Often there is very little space to be individuals in this kind of situation. In more extreme cases, this 'neediness' can even become abusive and obsessive. It can dominate the relationship and be destructive. This can feel like they are being 'checked up on' although this is often not seen by the one needing the reassurance.

These behaviours in a relationship create a great deal of pressure and intensity. The fear of rejection or someone being unhappy with you drives this behaviour and again leads you on someone else's path rather than your own.

The 'neediness' drives unnatural expectations which are difficult to maintain, and each person is left unhappy. The need to be loved or accepted has taken over the fun and natural path of the relationship. When we are looking for love to fulfil a deep-rooted need, then we are heading for a crash.

- Are you a person who would move mountains for others at the expense of yourself and your own life?
- Are you at another person's beck and call, dropping everything and running to be with them when they ask?
- Do you limit your plans, just in case there is a chance to be together or you are needed?
- Do you believe if you aren't there, your partner will be unhappy or end the relationship?

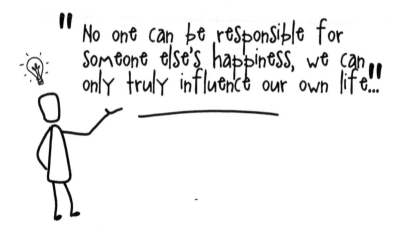

"No one can be responsible for someone else's happiness, we can only truly influence our own life..."

When we are trying to gain approval, we are often trying too hard to second-guess what the other person would want and then we bend over backwards to deliver.

This is like 'mind reading', which of course is an impossible quest. How can anyone know what the best thing for another is, certainly when using guesswork only? If our minds are spinning round trying to work out what we should do to 'make' our partner, friend, colleague or parent happy, then we are going to be emotionally drained. We will continue to wind ourselves up and can often feel out of control, as no one else can settle these fears, it has to come from within.

Insecurity

It's a human fact that we are wired with a desire to belong, be accepted and wanted. We fear being seen in a critical way, being isolated and being lonely. When there is an imbalance in our emotional, internal world, we live in fear, quite often a fear of rejection. This being one of our deepest human concerns. It is then that irrational thinking takes over and we are likely to react in an erratic or damaging way. Interestingly, both the victim and the persecutor roles are caught up commonly in these situations.

Emotional insecurity is a feeling of general unease or nervousness that may be triggered by perceiving that we are vulnerable or inferior in some way. It can be a sense of vulnerability or instability which threatens our self-image. This plays out the most in intimate relationships although can be there in other relationships.

Naturally when there is a sense of fear and insecurity, we will adopt a survival position which forces behaviours to be extreme and often irrational. This survival position is likely to be a combination of the persecutor and the victim.

Insecurity can be created in the very early days by: being raised in a chaotic, unpredictable environment; dealing with lack of self-belief due to never being accepted by others; having an unrealistic list of rules and expectations prescribed by significant others; not receiving positive reinforcement and encouragement; or feeling overshadowed and overlooked.

Certain situations or relationships in adult life can then trigger these deep-rooted fears developed in childhood. Having said that, people can develop these kind of insecurities from situations that happen as adults too. In these kind of situations, there can be an instant default button to over-protect, self-sabotage or blame ourselves or another and neither get us anywhere.

This can play out in day to day situations. Simply your partner doesn't text good night and this can be misinterpreted as they are seeing someone else or you have done something wrong. Because the fear chemicals are pumping through the mind, irrational thinking starts. This can be in the form of jealousy and ideas that the other person is being unfaithful.

The way the mind is programmed, the underlying thought can have you believing something quite irrational. For example, after a slight disagreement there is a fear that someone will end a relationship or be taken by another. The negative beliefs and fears that drive these 'made-up' thoughts that something bad is going to happen feel very real at the time and will cause drama within the relationship.

We have probably all been insecure and also have known others who are. Often, changes have been made to alleviate and minimise situations that trigger the other person's behaviour - not going to social events or cancelling arrangements with our friends just to have an easier time. These changes, while can offer some sort of relief, are not really the answer in the long run.

In these situations, the need to be reassured and comforted can become a big focus for the relationship. The insecurity can become like a third person in the relationship that needs constant attention. It can take up hours of time and energy and often the reassurance only lasts for a brief time. The spotlight needs to be switched to the insecure one rather than the whole relationship, as both partners are not taking responsibility and living the life they want.

Let's have a look at a case study to explain this kind of scenario.

Ruth and Scott are in a relationship. Scott has issues with trust and believes that Ruth is constantly going to finish the relationship and find someone else. Ruth hardly sees her friends now and is also very careful who she spends time with. She spends a lot of time reassuring Scott when she is going out or when he is particularly unsettled. She makes excuses or cancels arrangements at the last minute for an easier life. Ruth has become terrified of the negative response and arguments if she does her own thing - she is not getting on with her own life. She has to build herself up to tell him that she has been invited out with her friends, fearing the consequences.

The reality is not helping Scott. The insecurities are ruling all parts of their relationship. He is not addressing the root of his insecurities or at least acknowledging that he has a problem. He is expecting Ruth to be with him at all times so that he feels safe.

They spend hours on the phone when apart Ruth usually reassuring Scott as he is interpreting actions through his fear thinking. It is his responsibility to address his doubt rather than Ruth's responsibility to change her life or walk on eggshells to keep him happy.

Instinct versus insecurities

It is worth noting here that we are talking about something very different to our instinct. Sometimes fears and doubts are warranted because something is happening. We wouldn't want to ignore our instinct, our 'gut feeling'. Some people talk about just knowing that something isn't right. This is quite different to the fears driven by limiting beliefs in our mind. These are not connected to the outside world and usually made up because they are coming from a place of insecurity.

Social media

We need to just acknowledge the impact that social media is having on our mental health and relationships. Social media platforms such as Facebook and Instagram, have a big role to play in modern life insecurities. It has given people a platform for sharing their lives minute by minute and there can be a gulf between the assumptions we make and the truth. If we use this as a benchmark for our lives, it can create confusion and unhappiness. Before the internet, we were connected with people in a different way. We physically saw people and had contact with close or local friends but not a wider group, some of whom we don't really know.

In the world of social media we are connected with a massive circle. We can 'friend' or 'unfriend'! This can cause distress and trigger insecurities. A simple photograph posted with a stranger or a member of the opposite sex can lead to insecurity and jealousy, without any information or details. Social media can also paint an edited, exaggerated or distorted version of people's lives, which can cause loneliness, unhelpful comparisons and sadness. We have already explored the human habit of comparing ourselves to others. With social media, risk of comparing ourselves and our lives has never been greater, and we are yet to fully understand the impact.

Responsibility - saying 'sorry'

We teach children to say 'I'm sorry' very early on and as adults we spend less time thinking about the impact of our behaviour. Some refuse to apologise or don't see that there is any reason to do so. The polar opposite is that some say sorry for absolutely everything. Neither are taking true responsibility. Only true responsibility creates harmony and happiness.

Differing expectations are often at the root of situations and there can be confusion about another person's behaviour. Sometimes people don't feel they need or should say sorry and this can lead to becoming defensive; it may be connected to pride or an effort to protect their fragile sense of self (perpetrator).

It may be that some people find it difficult to separate their actions from their character. So if they did something bad, then they must be a bad person. If they have been neglectful, then they are uncaring or selfish. Saying sorry opens up the guilt and shame, which makes them feel bad about their actions and bad about themselves. Taking responsibility can feel too huge, as saying sorry would put them into a vulnerable position.

On the other hand, some people say sorry too often and for things which are not their fault. For absolutely everything. By misinterpreting and distorting situations, they find themselves automatically apologising - 'It must be me' or 'It's bound to be my fault'. When someone takes this level of responsibility, they will be weighted down. This may be unwarranted as no actual wrong has been committed. Being locked into this behaviour can lead to isolation and confusion because they believe that they can't get anything right.

Defensiveness

It is natural to want to protect ourselves although becoming defensive isn't really protection. When this is out of hand we may find ourselves in persecutor behaviour. Sometimes it can be justified if you are being accused of something a million miles from the truth. However, shifting quickly to defensiveness is a sign that you are in fight mode, which is highly unproductive and leads to irrational actions. As we have established, this can stem from living with criticism or always being put right, believing that we are always wrong and therefore on red alert to anything which triggers the past. Defensiveness can come across as insecure, closed-minded and aggressive.

An example could be when someone is dealing with a challenging situation but they feel like the other person is not being supportive. The other person is consumed with their own stuff and when challenged, rather than saying, 'Sorry, yes, I have been a little pre-occupied,' they turn it round and move to blame. This can cause unrest and unhappiness.

The blame games

There is a balance to master between accepting our part of responsibility in any given situation and passing that responsibility to someone else. Falling into the trap of taking the full blame every time is not helpful, it's damaging and allows others to not take responsibility for their part. On the other hand, it is not a good position to only blame the other person. The blame culture can be prolific in relationships, families, workplaces and within society too. It is quite a balancing act to get this right, although it can be a game changer. If we all learned how to get comfortable with taking the right level of responsibility, situations and challenges would be resolved and all parties would feel settled.

Unfortunately, over generations people have a leaning towards always blaming something or someone. It's as if we are conditioned into this type of thinking. This happens all around us and its evident that the media is blame-orientated. We can all find ourselves doing it in one way or another. We can blame someone for something not working out and an extreme would be blaming someone else for the way your life has turned out. We can be too quick to look for a scapegoat rather than looking within.

The blame games mean we are not taking responsibility; we are just passing the buck. We are on the drama triangle. Someone or something else - your husband, mother-in-law, neighbour, the media, the government or the dog - is to blame for the problem! This can appear in both the persecutor or victim positions.

We can get trapped in a habit of blaming others rather than taking full ownership. In these instances, you are focused externally and saying 'he said/she said or 'he did/she did'. This often means you are locked into the details of the situation and generally repeating the cycle. The relationship or situation will continually be in trouble with constant unrest or misunderstandings. Each person is adamant that the other person is at fault.

In some situations, there may be some truth in that, of course. One of the people in the relationship may be doing something that is unacceptable or causing problems, although the growth still lies with both identifying their part rather than just blaming. Without this reflection, it is frustrating as these situations will keep playing out and generally cause hurt, upset, confusion, or annoyance. As with any behaviours, once we are aware it is happening we are on our way to an alternative.

For example, do you blame the way your parents are for your relationship problems or do you blame your boyfriend for making you feel insecure? Looking at yourself, noticing and understanding how we have been programmed is much more effective than blaming others.

"Reflect now, is there a situation where you blame someone else?..."

In many instances, blame can feel like it brings some solace or consolation. It can feel like we are justified to blame someone else although being stuck with this is the damaging part. We can be consumed with pointing the finger at another or others, passing the responsibility, and this can feel satisfying, for a while. As with criticism, there can be a moment of gratification and justification because we can transfer the accountability away from ourselves.

The question is does it actually create fulfilment and, if so, for how long? The reality is that there is no personal responsibility for the blamer and therefore no room for personal development. Often we are in the resit class as there is something new to learn about ourselves although we are usually quick to blame. The risk, of course, is to the relationship itself and a likely conflict.

Let's take a look at a case study of what happens when we blame others or, in fact, when we are blamed constantly:

CASE STUDY

Liz was brought up with two older brothers and described it as an average childhood. She did however feel that there was a lack of obvious love in the house and she now understands this to have been more like conditional love. If she did well or pleased her parents, there was some praise, although there was a lot of attention on areas where she struggled. Her parents brought their children up to have standards, morals and values, although there was still a lack of emotional support. She often felt unsure about how to express her feelings as these were minimised in the past and never talked about.

Liz spent years blaming her parents for her relationship problems and how she had found it difficult to feel secure in relationships. She had been needy and terrified of rejection. While her feelings about herself will have been affected by the way she was brought up, there is no mileage in blaming her parents. There is no resolution or answers in this although there is in understanding why she behaves the way she does.

Liz recognised that when she moved away from blame and challenged the limiting beliefs about herself as not being true, she was able to create her own path in life.

The blame language

Let's have a look at the language common with blame - 'He makes me feel so angry' or 'She makes me feel like I am not good enough'. Even though someone else's behaviour can cause distress or upset, keep in mind no other person can actually make you feel anything. You are giving away your own power when you allow someone else to affect you in a damaging way. You have a choice, a decision as to how you will respond to others.

When you are happy in someone's company, you are still choosing to feel happy. The power is within all of us to choose to feel any emotion, at any time, and while the other person may create a situation which is part of it, the choice is still with you. With self awareness and control of your thoughts, you get to choose the response.

In more challenging situations, it can be warranted, acceptable and appropriate to respond with anger or getting upset. It is ok to have a reaction, however, the skill is to check that you do not stay in drama about the situation. Ensure not to allow yourself to continue to be consumed with the negative feeling. Believe it or not, you are choosing to hold on to the negativity if it continues much after the incident.

When you keep running the scenario in your mind, either what you or the other person did or didn't do, you are keeping the upset alive and using up energy.

For example, a family member might not acknowledge a gift you have sent. You feel annoyed, even angry and interpret this to mean that they are ungrateful. You blame them for 'making you feel' like this. This person doesn't have this power over you and therefore is not making you feel anything. You are allowing their action to affect you.

" When we move away from blame and take personal responsibility, " we increase our own power...

The result of this is finding we are riddled with anger, resentment and bitterness towards the 'blamed one' - this can feel like being stuck in a 'valley of blame'. Deep-rooted grudges can last a lifetime. We believe that it is 'their fault' and this unhappiness can be endured for years. In many situations, both parties end up feeling misunderstood and unheard. Living with this resentment and bitterness hurts the holder and creates more unhappiness and conflict.

We can get hung up on waiting, wanting and even expecting them to respond differently. Living in the past in these situations holds us back from healing and moving on.

Punishing others

We have already explored self-punishment, so now we will look at the reasons associated with punishing others. Punishing creates a relationship where there is control and a sense that someone is 'in charge'. It is behaviour frequently seen when someone is in a position of persecutor. It is usually linked to the person feeling unsettled in themselves or a feeling of no control. This can be past or present. They try to control and/or hurt someone else when they are hurting, desperate, feeling guilt, shame, or plainly unhappy.

Punishing others can be displayed in many ways, including giving the silent treatment, constantly putting people down and only seeing bad in them. The negative impact of this is obvious and is linked to people believing their comments are true, particularly over time.

Being right

Sometimes we can become fixed and closed to seeing someone else's way, trying to persuade another that we are right, and they are wrong. This can lead to years of arguing and coercing. A person will not back down because their motivation is that they want – even need – to be right. They will often need to have the last word, are certainly thinking in a very narrow way and are unable to accept, hear or consider another option. As with many behaviours, this is often out of their awareness, has become the norm and a habit.

"Peace is better than being right!!"

In some cases, the desire or need to be right helps them to manage an unconscious insecurity which they are unable or unwilling to address. They can put themselves above others and can find themselves adamant that the other person is wrong to appease their own insecurities. However, sometimes being right has a high price to pay. When we can't win, it can completely knock us and cause anger on the outside but often doubt inside. Either way this is a negative situation and traps us. The narrow thinking will prevent us taking a step back and considering what it might be like in the other person's shoes.

Another similar behaviour is where people always make every situation about themselves. This can be coupled with being right but every conversation leads back to them and their experiences. It often doesn't matter what is spoken about there will always be a response which is either better or the opposite, worse. They have suffered or achieved to a greater degree. These behaviours are also often linked to a sense of insecurity and doubt.

Quite often internal negative beliefs have been triggered and the need to be defensive and protect will be 'awoken'. In these instances, being right becomes a mission. Both parties are equally determined to be right, the conversation can turn into putting each other down or saying hurtful comments to feel better, neither creating a joyful experience.

When you become more aware of the flow of conversations and particularly challenging ones, then you have an opportunity to make changes. Paying attention allows you to notice who is dominating, who is trying to always be right or who turns everything to be about them.

- What is your normal pattern in a conversation?

- Do you passively give in, let the other person be right and blame yourself?

- Or do you continue the fruitless fight to be right?

More often than not, these situations usually create further misunderstandings, misinterpretations and communication breakdown. Interestingly, often the reason for conflict is purely that you both have a different opinion or approach to the situation and that each is unable to see from another's perspective. In most cases, there isn't a right or a wrong, it is just a differing view, and yet not accepting this causes conflict and drama.

Relationships and communication

Relationships with ourselves and others are our most complex undertaking in life. Each can be equally challenging. It's important to focus on good communication, mindful interpretation and appreciation of others. Before we move on to the next chapter, it will be useful to say a little more about our relationships with significant others and how our past can impact on our interactions.

When things go wrong in a relationship, we are often trapped in a cycle of unhelpful analysis, as though we are watching a TV programme on repeat and keeping the pain alive. The mind keeps old stories, scenarios and conversations circulating, and many people relive and regurgitate painful stories, spending hours analysing the 'What if...?' 'If only'... or 'How could they?' There is very little personal growth or peace in this thinking pattern, as every time we speak or think about the upset or negativity, the harm continues. These situations take up head space, use up energy and attention, which then affects our behaviour.

When a relationship ends, how many of us have spent time going over what happened, locked into the details of what was said or done, or focusing on what the other person is doing now? Today's prevalence of social media makes it so tempting to look them up and recreate the discomfort, again and again!

Many of the difficulties we experience are related to communication in our relationships. It is common to hear –'there was a breakdown in communication', 'we hardly communicate how we feel' or 'It is as if he/she is talking another language'.

Poor communication can manifest itself into misunderstandings and misinterpretation. This can happen in any kind of relationship although there tends to be a difference depending on who we are talking too. We may talk differently to our parents as adults; our parents are likely to talk to their 'adult children' in a certain way; certainly in intimate relationships; and different again with other family members, friends and work colleagues. Any poor communication will lead to frustration, unhappiness and confusion.

You complete me

Frequently in relationships, when a limiting self-belief is running the show, there can be a reliance on someone else to complete your identity and 'make you happy'. This not only puts a great deal of pressure on the relationship but is also giving away an enormous amount of personal power. We can be governed by our need for security, approval, recognition and acceptance. How many people feel that being in a relationship or having loads of friends completes them - could this be you or someone you know? Many people place their own happiness dependent on another person or a situation changing. This is a fragile position to be in. We can fall into a trap of believing that everything will be fine when something happens. It is common to hear people saying that everything will be fine when.....

- 'Everything will be good when I have a boyfriend'

- 'Everything will be fine when we are married'

- 'Everything will be ok when we live together'

- 'Everything will be ok when we move house' - and the list goes on.

When you rely heavily on someone else or something changing, this is not only pressure, but a huge risk of a let-down. Other people or a situation do not have this power, it can only come from within. While a person or a change of circumstance can enhance your life, it is not the deep answer.

How many times have you been feeling so insecure, unhappy and miserable and then someone, usually that significant other, sends a text or calls and you feel instantly ok again? In the time before this call, your mind is racing with negative thoughts either about yourself or them. There is a risk your mind will be catastrophising and making up all sorts of irrational thoughts. Now, while it is great to have that initial feeling of happiness after receiving their message, it is not a safe place to be. It means that you are not 'self assured'. The real danger of relying on others is that they are quite likely to let you down without even realising. If you are relying on someone else to make you happy then there is an issue.

Seeking external reassurance and love without having internal resources is a recipe for problems. This may result in picking the wrong person, because there is a belief that you are fulfilled when in a relationship. In these scenarios having a relationship is what matters rather than checking other important parts of the compatibility. We can even do this with friendships and find ourselves putting up with negative behaviours. The limiting beliefs are driving the need to be secure with someone else and unless managed you are likely to attract someone not necessarily right for you. This is a doubly risky position.

There is a high chance that you will be disappointed and then - crash! If you are relying on someone or something else to bring you happiness, you are more than likely not believing in yourself enough. There needs to be self-love and self-acceptance first.

"How often do you look outside for the questions and answers for our problems?..."

The saying goes that you need to love yourself before you can love someone else. If you are not happy within yourself and you are relying on someone else to make you happy, there is huge expectation and responsibility placed on the other person. This can make them run for the hills or the relationship simply will not work due to the pressure and expectations. The goal is to be happy within and then any relationship, friendship or an occasion can enhance that happiness, not the other way around.

Making assumptions

Another reality within human behaviour is making assumptions and these also can cause challenges within relationships. While it is normal and required to make some assumptions, it is worth putting our attention on the negative aspect which affect our lives. Assumptions are when we believe things are a certain way with little or no evidence that show we are correct. These can become a dangerous game and can often create challenges. Our minds presume that our beliefs are true and use them to interpret the world around us.

In general terms, we craft these assumptions to make sense of where we are, what we are about and what is happening. We make judgements, form interpretations and come to conclusions based on the beliefs or ideas we have formed. For example, in a previous relationship were deceit and trust became an issue, a new relationship your partner call to cancel a coffee because of work your mind jumps to an immediate conclusion that something is wrong.

In life, we have to make a reasonable level of assumptions; this is normal and is happening constantly, day to day. However, it's so easy to 'think we know' what is going on in someone else's head and to imagine that we understand why a person has taken a particular course of action. We don't really know but we make a guess based on our imagination, past experiences or wishful thinking. This is where the danger lies. We start to second guess and mind read what is happening.

In the same way that we place limiting beliefs on ourselves, it also works the other way - when we believe something about someone else, it doesn't necessarily make it true. We are all guilty of mind reading, jumping to conclusions and making things up about other people and their behaviour. This happens because it fits with our internal view of the world and specifically that situation. The problem with making these assumptions is that often we are wrong. We incorrectly assume that a person has a particular motivation for their actions or that an event took place for a specific reason. This becomes our truth.

Can you think when you last made an assumption that became a challenge for you? Maybe when someone cancelled a dinner arrangement, you assumed that it must be something you had done, despite there being no evidence of this. Maybe your boss asked, 'Can I have a word?' and you assumed instantly that you must have done something wrong or even veered into the extremes of thinking you were getting the sack.

Some assumptions are trivial; others are potentially devastating as we can confuse them with the truth. Instead of using the facts, we prefer to make judgements based on our emotions, beliefs, expectations and hopes. We then make these our reality.

In relationships, it may be that you think someone isn't into you because they haven't been in touch? The doubt creeps in and you assume that the non-contact equals 'they don't like me'. This can happen in both sexes, although it does appear to be more prevalent with women. This could be because men appear to find it easier to compartmentalise their thoughts. Generally, men are good at being in the 'work mode' and then in 'leisure mode', whereas women generally merge the different aspects of their lives. This is not intended to be a sexist comment; generally women are just more likely to think about a number of things at the same time, whereas men tend not to do that as much. For example, men are less likely to think about their relationship while at work. This can come as a surprise to a woman when they ask if their man has thought about an unresolved issue during the day and the man replies 'Haven't given it any thought.' This can be misinterpreted as they don't care, but that is probably not the reality.

As a result, many people create a false reality about what is happening and make decisions based on that assumption. We rarely stop for a sanity check on our perception; this is why coaching and chatting with a friend works as they provide another perspective on the issue. We assume that our partners, friends or close family members understand us and the intended meaning is loud and clear when we communicate. We get frustrated when they don't 'get it' or 'get us'. In fact, ladies, this is where we have to own up to something. Many are guilty of becoming irritated when our partners or family members don't understand the meaning behind our words. For example, we say, 'I'm FINE' and then get annoyed when this is interpreted as everything is ok, when clearly it is not! Communication is a fine art and when managed carefully, with thought and a lack of negative, drama-based emotion, it will make a huge difference.

How are you reacting?

Let us come back to our response to others' actions or a situation. Do you find yourselves worried, upset or anxious because of someone else's behaviour? It could be something as simple as they haven't phoned, and the situation has triggered massive emotions within. We tend to make up a false reality, don't take time to stop and check if there is real evidence to back up our thinking or consider if there is another perspective.

" Is what you are thinking really happening?... "

We can jump to conclusions, creating negative thoughts about a situation, distorting the reality and turn it back onto ourselves. The mind can start to run with negative thoughts like 'I am not good enough' or 'I don't deserve to be happy'. The intense reaction is an indicator that something is amiss within you and often your response becomes unwarranted to the situation. The thoughts and behaviours become more erratic and irrational, in drama. You could be constantly phoning or texting and your emotional response to them not picking up is inappropriate. You feel anxious and make all kinds of things up in your head.

A situation may have arisen when you felt hurt, your emotions are uncontrollable, so you constantly let the other person know or dwell on it. These behaviours need to be reined in as they are exhausting for everyone and can destroy the relationship. The truth is your behaviours are more likely to be driven by your own thinking and could be triggering insecurities and doubt. This response could be a message that you should be doing something differently. If you notice and change your thoughts, the shift in focus will make a difference.

When you start to take responsibility, you can decide what you would like to happen. Wouldn't it be better to be able to settle and soothe yourself when someone changes a plan or doesn't act as you had expected rather than heading for a meltdown? Also, it is much better to move away from believing that someone else is ruining or taking over your life, or to notice that someone else has way too much control. Just to clarify again, I am not saying that we have to accept other people's poor behaviour. For example, if someone is constantly cancelling or changing arrangements, then we can feel upset or annoyed initially. If someone is being moody and uncooperative, you are not expected to accept this. However, start to take control and put a different kind of attention on scenarios when your automatic response is highly emotional, self-deprecating or you assume it is because of you. You will notice a difference.

Assumptions about reactions

We can make assumptions about how we expect people close to us to react to a situation - they may always criticise, 'kick-off' because of insecurity, or be in a grumpy mood when asked to change plans. We unconsciously prepare for a response we are expecting. Although anticipating and preparing to a point makes sense, it isn't a healthy approach as this can affect the outcome. It is as if we are observing every response through a microscope, waiting for that same reaction and, when we are looking for it, we are causing tension and possibly contributing to the pattern being repeated.

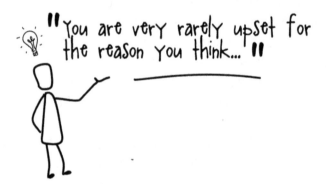

"You are very rarely upset for the reason you think..."

Remember Peter and Wendy in the example earlier. Wendy may have often expected for Peter to have a problem, based on previous situations, and therefore acted in a certain way herself. She may become frustrated or dismissive of him or overcompensated to alleviate the situation. Peter expected himself to be a certain way and then interpreted her behaviour as a reinforcement of his assumptions that he was no fun to be with or a nuisance.

Much of these responses just seem to happen to us, an auto pilot, having no chance to 'think' and process the situation rationally. In these situations, emotions are usually running high and therefore clear, rational thinking is lacking. In a difficult conversation, generally each person isn't listening to the other properly which causes more distress - and can be triggered by a fairly minor thing.

A variation of the following scenario is all too common in relationships and so it is important to recognise and separate your own behaviour and that of others. Here is a case study to explain more:

CASE STUDY

Caroline and Chris have just started dating. Chris has been hurt in a past relationship and hasn't got serious with anyone since. He likes Caroline and is keen for this one to work. Caroline has also had a few relationships and is very clear that she will not be messed around again. She has been in quite controlling relationships before and is therefore on red alert for any similar behaviour.

Chris quickly realises that he is not feeling happy. Caroline is a strong, independent woman and, while he is attracted to this, he is ultimately not feeling in control. He jumps to conclusions that she is not bothered about him, doesn't prioritise him and he feels she talks down to him.

What happened here is that through Chris' limiting beliefs that he is not good enough, his memories from the past have been triggered and he feels uncomfortable. He is moody and aggressive as he blames Caroline for 'making him feel unwanted'. Caroline, on the other hand, is uncomfortable with this kind of behaviour as she is not free in the relationship and is constantly worried that there is going to be an argument. Chris starts to resent Caroline's friendships and her outgoing personality. He starts to believe that she doesn't want to be with him and that she will be looking elsewhere. His negative thinking is taking over and dominating his thoughts, which is feeding his actions. Ultimately neither are happy or fulfilled.

Moving forward

You can never truly be happy when you build your happiness on what others do, say or think about you. Happiness comes from within.

We have been exploring what lies deep within many of us and what prevents us from having the life that we want. We have identified many of the common behaviours and the impact of self-limiting beliefs. As mad it is seems, these can become your comfort blanket.

The secret of happiness is to work out how to be and become the 'real you'. The answer is not with someone else or allowing them to have a position of power. If you are spending too much time trying to make others happy then you are probably not being yourself or looking after yourself. If you are spending time and energy trying to second guess and then overcompensating to gain approval or attention, you will not be following your own path.

Your hidden self or inner child is likely to be responding with irrational and highly emotional behaviours. If you can take a step back, look through a different lens and notice those unhealthy responses and behaviours, you can see your inner self. You can then take charge rather than blaming others.

This chapter has put the focus on becoming self aware. We have fast-tracked your awareness. Now we will explore how you can change what you have noticed. That which you don't like or want, let go of the old habits and travel on the next part of your journey.

This kind of change may feel unachievable, but have faith that there is always a different route. Some of you will need professional coaching for this to happen, although anyone can start to challenge their negative thinking themselves and watch for the impact. As said in the first chapter, we are way more powerful than we know. So, take the next step and move away from blame, take responsibility and continue on your own path. When you become aware of what you are doing and why, it gets exciting to know that you do have the control to change it.

CHAPTER FIVE

Changing the Mould

Changing the mould

We have been exploring the many factors which created and shaped the mould as to who we all are. It is inevitable that we mirror and learn 'how to be' because of so many aspects of our lives, from both our own experiences and those with others. We influence and shape each other throughout our lives, yet everything that we have learnt doesn't have to stay, particularly the behaviours that are unhelpful. We often don't stop and look at ourselves and just keep going along knowing that it isn't quite right. 'This is how I have always been' does not have to be your mantra.

This chapter will go through how you can make some positive changes, reduce negativity and nurture that self-belief. By doing this you can open yourself up to new possibilities and start to be the best version of yourself.

Like water moving down a stream, we change constantly. We are responding in every moment and all situations can and will influence us - even the weather! Our mood can be affected by so many outside influences, particularly other people and, importantly, by our own internal response being triggered constantly.

Once we have noticed the patterns, habits and behaviours that form within us, then we can start to break the mould. Often this requires us to be truly honest with ourselves, which can be a challenge (and even scary).

In the spirit of being honest, are you proud of your own behaviours at times or do you feel embarrassed about how you react? When you put a spotlight on private behaviours and thoughts, reflect, aim to move away from blame, and take responsibility, then you can make changes.

A place to start is to take some pressure off yourself by recognising that it's not your fault, it's not anyone's fault. By learning how to train your subconscious mind, you can control your behaviour, break bad habits, get rid of unwanted emotions and fix your belief system.

So, are you ready to create a new path?

4 Steps to The New Way

There are so many ways to tackle the challenges in our powerful minds. We will focus on 4 key areas which will help to break the barriers that restrict you and then guide you towards discovering a new and clearer path. This ultimately means you can change the future, regardless of what has happened before.

Each step will move you forward in a different way, although they are all ultimately linked. Any exercise or approach can be done independently, although mixed together you will achieve a greater result. The exercises are chosen to be simple and can be put into practice easily. There are case studies to help explain different scenarios. They are all designed to help you take control of your life.

The 4 Steps to The New Way are:

- **Awareness**

- **Letting go**

- **Reframing**

- **The power of language**

Start to PICTURE yourself in a.... NEW WAY...

Awareness

Step 1 is to understand the importance of becoming more aware and learning how to achieve it. It's about paying really close attention to yourself and becoming more alert to your unhelpful behaviours and unwarranted responses. This is a big part of making any changes, probably about 80% believe it or not. When you dare to admit to yourself that things could be better, then this is a motivator to change the path.

Before we begin exploring what habits and behaviours we need to notice, let's firstly start with a very quick and simple exercise, a mini body scan. This is a mindfulness exercise and will help you to be in the moment. It helps you become grounded and we do this by focusing on the body and the breathe. It helps you see how busy the mind is. It allows you to notice what is happening, being present while giving the mind something to do. It is a skill to master with a lot of practice.

The benefits

This exercise is useful to start or end the day. It can also be used when the mind feels particularly busy, you feel anxious or confused. This will help to build up resilience and strength from within, while giving you a few moments of calmness away from your own thoughts.

There are many mindfulness exercises out there and making this a regular part of your day is recommended for mental health, physical and psychological reasons.

STEP to CHANGE

Being in the moment

Being in the moment

Let's have a go at being in the moment with this simple exercise.

If you would prefer to listen to this exercise, it can be found on www.2-minds.co.uk/body-scan/. You only need a couple of minutes to do it and you can repeat as many times as you like.

...........Take a seat. With eyes closed or just half-closed, allow your attention to rest on your experience of your body in the chair.

Notice the areas of contact between your body and the chair. Notice the support the chair is offering to you right now. Become aware that the chair is supporting your body by carrying most of your physical weight.

Allow this to happen. Allow a comfortable sense of heaviness to spread through your body, supported and carried by the chair. Then notice the rise and fall of the breath. Notice any tension you are holding within your body, the head, neck, shoulders, down the arms. Notice any tension in your chest and abdomen. Notice any tension in your back, down the spine, into your buttocks, legs, ankles and feet.

Each time you notice any tightness or difficulty in these different parts of your body allow it to drain into your chair, be absorbed by your chair. Just rest as you are supported by the chair for a few minutes.

Curiosity

Getting curious about your behaviour and noticing familial habits puts you in a different place. When you can spot and admit that you are being held back by something, probably a self-belief or a story from the past, you can make a change. When your relationships are forming a pattern and not working out, you can consider what is buried deep within that needs your attention.

Just for clarity, being aware doesn't entail over-analysing, over-thinking or being paranoid. These behaviours are the ones you want to move away from. Instead, you want to notice your own reactions to situations and the accompanying thoughts. These reactions can become habitual and become a part of us. You are looking out for any negative behaviours, ones like automatic negative thinking, people pleasing, jumping to conclusions or adopting the blame position.

We will start to break some of these down and you can check in as to whether these feel familiar to you.

Broken record

Generally, we spend a lot of time 'being in our heads'. When we have repetitive thoughts spinning round and round, this usually leads to frustration, confusion or even anger.

Or we might find ourselves consumed with emotions, like sadness or anxiety and this feels out of control. It then becomes difficult to focus on anything else and affects concentration, enjoyment, and, for some people, keeps them awake at night.

Often the kind of things we keep on repeat are how we handled a situation or how someone else has been. It might be if someone has said something you have heard as a criticism, made a negative comment, behaved badly (in your eyes), ignored you or challenged you. In our minds, we are constantly running over 'what if' or trying to work out what to say or do next. This 'broken record' thinking prevents us from coming up with anything useful, new or is far from inspiring. We look for a quick fix and tend to focus externally rather than on us. This is quite exhausting and sometimes it is actually someone else's problem. Either way, the solutions are not there, and the focus is off us. It can feel like the mind is stuck or out of control.

When you minimise any negative internal chatter, you will have a clearer mind to think and see a situation differently and probably more innovatively. Realising that we are not our thoughts, or our emotions, is freeing.

Internal sat nav

Our internal 'sat nav' guides us to let us know whether we are on the right path or not. As we have said one of the mind's jobs is to protect and we all know the signals that give us a feeling that something isn't right. Quite often we ignore them or jump to blaming someone or something else for our discomfort rather than be self-reflective.

When we regularly or, in some cases, constantly feel unsettled, we need to be able to see this differently. It is often an alarm resonating in our bodies and a message from the mind. It is usually there because we are not doing what is right for us. We can then distort a situation or associate it with something external. These alarms became more and more sensitive as our beliefs and self-esteem take a battering. We often mistake the discomfort as being associated with the other person's behaviour or reaction rather than something we can change ourselves.

Our responses, like anxiety, anger or sadness, can suddenly appear, almost like coming out of the blue. It could be a stomach churn, a nauseous feeling or a doom sensation. These physical symptoms are often part of the internal world bringing our attention to something that we perceive as wrong or dangerous. It is these feelings that we often desperately want to avoid although it is so often a call to action and a wonderful lesson in disguise.

We can get so uncomfortable that we want to run away or feel the need to fight back. While this is a natural response, avoiding the situation or being angry towards another may mean that a personal lesson is missed. When we miss our lesson, there is a high chance that similar situations will be repeated until we do! Do you ever hear yourself saying 'Why does this keep happening to me'? It can become more and more painful and challenging each time - remember the 're-sit' class?

When you learn to sit with the uneasiness and not run away, you are more likely to see the insights, both positive and negative and can take a different viewpoint on the experience. A word of warning, this will feel like a stretch, particularly in very painful and harsh situations, although well worth it. Instead, move from a position of feeling sorry for yourself (victim position) or blaming (persecutor position) towards looking for the lessons available. These lightbulb moments are a gift and bring the most significant changes which can be transformational.

By changing our perspective and looking closely at ourselves then we can see more clearly. This could be something as simple as 'when my girlfriend is running late, what do I need to do for myself to be settled rather than losing it'? Remember, challenging situations and when there appears to be a mistake, these can be lessons in disguise. We can either beat ourselves up and feel devastated, or instantly blame others, or we can take it as an opportunity to improve.

Making more mistakes creates more feedback and an opportunity to learn more lessons. In many people's lives, unfortunately the biggest mistake that they make is not acknowledging the lesson. To move away from this type of thinking, look within and find out what you are doing or not doing which is causing you the issue.

It is far better to see each situation as an opportunity to grow and develop rather than consider it a disaster. Being mindful of your thinking and behaviours behind why you do certain things and noticing what triggers the emotional responses gives you a new platform. It is a clear signal that something needs to change.

Having courage

In this learning, we need to be courageous to admit our own flaws, particularly if we have been in the habit of blaming anyone and everyone for our unhappiness. We can feel extremely vulnerable and exposed when it is ourselves that are at the root of our own problems.

Once we are paying attention to ourselves and our internal world, then there may be a push and pull situation as we recognise and acknowledge the part we play in situations.

Although it can feel virtually impossible to see any good in awful situations, in most relationship type issues there will be something good we can take for ourselves. We must be brave to look though. Being honest with ourselves, even after something that was challenging at the time, can be so enlightening.

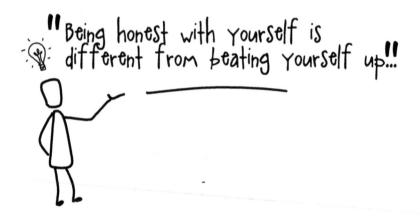

"Being honest with yourself is different from beating yourself up!!"

In these moments, we feel vulnerable and unsettled, something we usually want to avoid. Vulnerability is often seen as negative. It can be seen as shame, uncertainty, fear, disappointment or emotional exposure. In her book, The Power of Vulnerability, Brené Brown, American scholar, author, and public speaker says "The birthplace of vulnerability is creativity and innovation". We shy away from feeling afraid and vulnerable. When we can see weaknesses as a strength, then we are freer and on that new path.

Once out of the drama and after some reflection, we can often see things differently and certainly feel different. There may be a 'phew that was a close shave' or a recognition that it was for the best, even though at the time it was devastating. An example, you feel distraught after being dumped. Once your emotional mind has settled, you can see that it was a negative relationship which wasn't right for you. The dynamics between the two of you were destructive rather than positive. The progress will come from being able to accept what has happened, let go of any negativity and be patient while you recover and heal.

One sure way to get you moving towards being self-aware is to imagine that others are watching. Imagine yourself on a stage with an audience. Imagine someone being able to hear all your thoughts or see how you behave behind closed doors. Do this with whatever the behaviour or thoughts that you know aren't helpful. For example, you are constantly checking your phone if someone hasn't called, or you are off hand with a loved one. We often behave, think and feel in a certain way out of the public eye or ear. We usually only let our nearest and dearest see us at our most vulnerable or worst. We would rarely speak to a friend as bluntly and honestly as we sometimes speak to our loved ones. The task is to be focused on having the courage to be honest with yourself to be able to move forward.

Have a go at looking at some of your own thoughts and behaviours.

STEP to CHANGE

Changing your perspective

Changing your perspective

Take a moment to think about your own situation.

1)   Describe a situation that didn't work well for you

2) How did you feel e.g. angry, upset, confused

3) Consider this from a different perspective, what do you notice?

4) What did you learn for yourself?

Moving from negativity to positivity

By recognising the negative aspects of your life and behaviour you may notice some physical symptoms too. The medical world and alternative medicine acknowledge that many physical symptoms are a manifestation of an internal emotion or conflict. Negativity hurts us; it causes illness and saps our energy and motivation for life. We can experience physical pain (such as headaches, back pain or stomach pain) caused by emotional, mental and behavioural factors. This psychogenic pain is commonly connected with social rejection, a broken heart, grief, and other emotional events.

Anger, stress, frustration, guilt, fear, regret and sadness harm our bodies and cause illness. They affect our perception of the world and cloud our judgement. Negativity, conflict or upset affects our emotional, mental and physical self. What is seen or experienced in the physical body becomes a mirror of our inner world. Consider disease as 'dis-ease', a lack of peace, stillness and comfort.

In order to move from negativity towards positivity, we need to develop different muscles in the mind. We will use a metaphor for this, it is like going to the gym with your mind. It is here that we develop the muscles of a positive mind. Think of this, to get physically fit, we know we need to exercise regularly and build our muscles over time. This will take time, repetition and commitment.

Think of the mind as a big muscle. It needs a thorough exercise programme so that we can develop a reserve of resilience, confidence, self-respect, worthiness and determination. It needs to be strengthened over time, with repetition and commitment. The great secret here is you don't need to actually go to gym or a class, it can happen everywhere and anytime. All day, every day.

Instead of doing the old habit of focusing on negative things about yourself, past experiences and things you haven't done or got, focus on the good things in your life. It is writing the 'done list' rather than the 'to-do-list' or what you have rather than what you don't. You may not have the dream relationship yet, but you do have a great network of friends. These can be even the smallest things, particularly if life is a little challenging. When you acknowledge something good, even a lovely chat with a friend or a walk, then you will feel more settled. It doesn't necessarily change the bigger picture, but this tactic does help build positivity and resilience.

So instead of focusing on negativity, on what you haven't got or done, take the time to recognise and acknowledge your achievements, no matter how small. We are usually proficient at sharing proud moments of others, particularly children, although it is all too common to miss doing this with ourselves.

From today, take a positive approach to feeling proud of yourself and notice how it impacts on your motivation and energy. Acknowledge even the tiny steps as this will help you build up strength and resilience which will allow you to cope when the 'chips are down'.

This approach will move you towards a place of appreciation and gratitude. It sounds so simple and yet it is powerful. When you start to change your thinking and beliefs then you will get the life you know you deserve. Expect an abundance of positivity and good times.

Take yourself to your mind gym.

STEP to CHANGE

The mind gym

The mind gym

Take a moment to think about your own situation.

This is an exercise you can do regularly, even each day.

Note down three achievements , small or large:

1

2

3

Note down three times you made a good choice for yourself:

1

2

3

Note down three things you are grateful for

1

2

3

Note down three times when you have been kind to yourself

1

2

3

Determination

Determination is a specific part of our mind gym. To overcome some of life's challenges we need to dig deep for determination and courage. We need to consciously decide to do this 'stuff'. The old habits are ingrained so we must be determined to make the changes and go to the mind gym. It is common to start something well at the beginning and then slip back into old habits. It won't come to us easily and, more often than not, we are judging ourselves when we quit or think 'I can't be bothered'.

One example of pure determination all of us have been through is when we learned to stand and walk as a child. When we are learning to stand up or walk, we never give up or quit. We have all been there even if it is out of our conscious memory. Children show unquestionable determination, concentration and motivation when learning to walk. It is innate within us although there is nothing that will stop the child. He or she falls down time and time again and yet finds something inside to continue. Many of us quit on ourselves all the time although we are often not valuing our efforts and progression enough to succeed.

We all have this ability within us and yet we stop using these resources of resilience and determination in challenging areas of our lives.

What is success to you?

What is success to one person can be regarded a failure or shortcoming to someone else. Most people agree that success means achieving, accomplishing or reaching something that makes them feel content and fulfilled. Some people measure success by money, although money does not automatically equal life success, or indeed happiness.

" Quitters never win and winners never quit... "

The pace at which we achieve our success is also personal; the starting point is not the same for all and the journey we take to reach our goal can be varied, with many avenues and 'speed bumps' along the way. This makes measuring success, and therefore comparing it, impossible. We are all different and there can be a lot of pressure on what is perceived as being successful.

So, what about failure? Rather than seeing failure as a problem, we can talk about it differently. Success can be achieved by learning from your mistakes. We all have had challenges that shaped our lives, and through those challenges, we've grown. Just because we don't always achieve what we had hoped for does not mean we have failed. There will always be learning. We can have all the determination and motivation to move us forward, although one of the reasons we quit is because we are not clear on what it is we want. To recognise whether your internal 'sat nav' is taking you in the right direction, you need to have a good idea of where you want to be heading and what you are aiming for.

It is very common to feel unsettled in life and have no idea what it is you really want. The mind doesn't like it when it doesn't know and have certainty. You need to get clear on what it is you want and what it will be like when you have got it. This can be a small goal or stepping stone to a great achievement. What is vital is knowing what it is.

STEP to CHANGE

Your own success

Your own success

Take some time to think about these questions for you know what is happening for you.

Writing down your answers makes it more powerful.

Ask yourself:

What is it you would want to achieve?

What is preventing you from achieving that now?

What do you need to do to take steps towards this goal?

What will it be like when you have achieved your goal?

Patience

Alongside determination, there is often a need for the opposite; this is to be patient with yourself and others. This is particularly vital when it comes to creating change. Generally, humans have become impatient and therefore quite demanding. With the evolution of technology, we have become a society where everything happens instantly. We can buy anything on-line and have it delivered the next day, we can download something immediately and we can see the pictures we have taken that same moment. We want it as soon as we have decided we need it.

"Everything is happening at the perfect time..."

However, we need to take our time when it comes to personal growth and change. Commonly, we become frustrated when changes are not happening 'quickly enough' and yet making changes within ourselves, with our behaviours or habits, will take some time. We can't do it all and change ingrained behaviours overnight.

Personal growth is like the weather. In the short term, things can change rapidly and you can experience a lot of ups and downs. In the long term, however, personal growth is more like a gradual climate change. Practicing patience can allow us to step through those rainy days to get lasting results. Expecting your life to change in an instant will only lead to disappointment.

Let's look at how taking time out to reflect can help you create the changes you need in your life.

Reflection

When things are going wrong in life, particularly in relationships, there can be a tendency to want to fix whatever is happening immediately, or the complete opposite - to do nothing. We often want to shy away from any discomfort, and therefore rush to find a solution. Before now, an option may have been spending time defending yourself or blaming the other person, making your point and not backing down until you are right. Alternatively, you are so passive that the other person just walks all over you. A positive step in difficult times is to consider 'time out'.

Space or time out, time to be on our own and to reflect is vital. This can be something that some people are comfortable with, while others really struggle. Some people prefer to reflect alone, and others need to talk it through. Either way, this time away from the difficult situation is a necessity and something that many people, particularly in intimate relationships or within families, can benefit from.

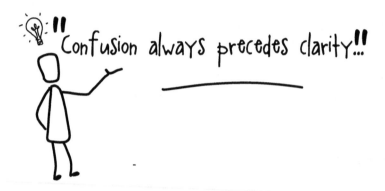

"Confusion always precedes clarity!!"

Being able to take time out is a great skill and where we learn the most. When we are immersed in a situation we are more likely to feel stuck. Many dread a partner, family member or friend saying, 'I need some space'. When limiting beliefs are lurking, this is often interpreted as 'They have had enough', 'It must be me' or a damning thought such as 'I am a horrible person' or 'I am not worthy'.

A real test is to sit with the discomfort of the situation and wait to see what unfolds. It can feel uncomfortable not knowing which way to turn and it can be difficult to deal with any uncertainty. Watch out for the tendency to dive straight back in!

Rushing with a big decision can often lead us down the wrong path and it's good to notice when we are doing just this. Noticing helps us to slow down and listen to our true self, leading us to the right path. Sometimes in the silence or break, we realise the most wonderful things about ourselves and can learn the greatest lessons. For example, we are good enough and, it is just the other person's approach to life that has made us doubt ourselves.

The space not only allows both parties to calm down, but helps to re-engage with a rational, sensible mind, rather than the emotional part of the mind. This part is upset and quite probably not listening. In many situations, there is often no actual right or wrong. There will be different approaches, viewpoints, ideas, expectations, interpretations and even more complex, different perceptions. Just in the same way we have different tastes and styles.

Space does, however, need to be managed well. Be mindful not to keep the negative situation alive by thinking about it repeatedly or talking about it constantly to others. By doing so you are choosing to keep putting yourself right into a negative place time and time again. You are reliving and going over who said or did what rather than looking for a new perspective for you. It is acceptable to have an initial, or occasional, vent to provide some relief and get it all out, though not for long and certainly not constantly.

The trick in many of these situations is not to jump back in too early before you have managed to heal or re-align yourself. Going back with the same thinking will create only the same outcome. The hardest option is to stay with yourself while you process what is happening and work out what you now need to do. It can be difficult to sit with the discomfort, whether that be sadness, anger or guilt and see what unfolds. It is enlightening if you are open to realising something different.

During this reflection time, we can feel like we are not getting anywhere. We can get in a state of confusion, and this can lead us to be too hasty. Sticking with it will give clarity though we need to add some patience to the mix. The goal is to be able to stay with the confusion and discomfort and know that there are good things coming, great and valuable insights about yourself.

During this time, we may need to dig deep and move towards trusting that the right direction or answer is coming. We need to believe that we can handle what happens to us, that we can find enough resilience from within and this is happening for a reason. This is possible when we are aware of what is happening and what we are doing. It is when we don't have awareness we actually get into a pickle. A great mantra to try is 'This time will pass', because it will.

STEP to CHANGE

Your own part

Your own part

Take a moment to think about your own situation.

Consider a situation that is bothering you at present. Rather than overthinking the detail of the story, try dropping the narrative 'he said/she did' and just sit back and reflect.

Allow your mind to focus on yourself. Be honest with yourself and notice if you can learn something about your own behaviour. You may notice that you have been doing too much of something or not enough of something else.

What behaviours are you:

Doing too much of (e.g. running around after others)

An example, a friendship has changed, and you are filled with negative thoughts and feelings. You feel like you have upset them, and this is churning you up inside. When you observe the situation from a quiet, solid place, something new might come to light.

You may realise that you have taken the situation too personally or that this friend was not being a true friend, or you have allowed something to happen which isn't healthy.

Not doing enough of (e.g. not prioritising self-care)

More choices

When we are self-aware and honest with ourselves then we are more likely to be taking responsibility and positive action. This new approach helps us to be more 'now' focused and dealing with our responses in the present. Technically there is actually only now and yet the mind complicates life by holding onto the past and worrying about the uncertainty of the future. The past is a series of memories we have stored. It is a version of the event and therefore often distorted somewhat. We all experience situations based on our internal world, so the memory is never the same as anyone elses. Being aware of what is happening in the mind changes everything. The future to the mind can become scary or it is something that you can embrace as you steer to create the future that you want.

With self-awareness in your armour, it is now time to look at Step 2 of the New Way - Letting Go.

Letting Go

Step 2 on this journey is the ability to let go. This can come with a range of responses. Letting go can feel like you are allowing someone or something to win and yet holding onto it is only harming you. We will never forget what has happened and holding onto it feels like you are in protection mode. The subconscious mind, as we have said, remembers everything by way of keeping us safe and yet hurt or anger from a past experience is only ever going to hold us back.

We will always remember the story, the situation, the relationship that has caused the issues, though the aim is to let go of the negativity associated with it. This can be negative or self-beating thoughts, strong negative emotions and learned behaviours or habits that are old, unhelpful and usually destructive.

It is not to be underestimated that this task is hard. The mind will want to keep us in fight or flight mode when you have been hurt. Being willing to let go of whatever is no longer necessary in our lives is quite a job. It is like the negativity and old story we tell become a comfort blanket and even though it is holding us back, we have come to believe that this is us. It is these thoughts that hold us back from shaping a confident, happy self and having a future with emotional freedom.

We know now that keeping old painful experiences alive is destructive. It is these stories, which have often been exaggerated or distorted, that we need to leave in the past as a set of memories rather than a living reality. This will mean that they no longer define you. Allowing them to be a comfortable part of the past (yes, even the horrendous ones) is far better than reliving them. And revenge will be less gratifying as we have a solution we can control.

When we can do this, we will then be less attached to viewing ourselves and life from the past. When we see ourselves through the lens of doom and failure, we will limit ourselves. More can be achieved when we see ourselves in a new way, identifying less and less as a victim. There are many different approaches to letting go, as it isn't quite as simple as just that. Let's have a look at a few options which will hopefully feel achievable.

Acceptance

One powerful approach to letting go is acceptance. Once we become aware of our own behaviour and accept what has happened, then we can begin to understand what we can learn from a situation, thus let go. It is, generally, normal to have had a reaction towards something difficult, what is not helpful is holding onto that reaction. When we accept a situation or our behaviour at the time, we will allow ourselves to move forward and let go of any negativity. Quite commonly we find ourselves frustrated with the situation and/or ourselves which is unhelpful. Keep in mind - there is no failure, just feedback.

When it comes to accepting others and their differences, this should be easy and yet isn't. We naively assume that everyone else thinks and sees everything like we do. We couldn't be more wrong. When it comes to accepting others, we need to be comfortable that there are other opinions and views, and then bring our attention back to our response. Quite often the other person is not going to change or see the situation any other way, so accepting and acknowledging this is important. We are then letting go of the need for them to see the situation our way and this becomes freeing. It certainly isn't our job to try and change anyone else. Our ability to accept others, even though we feel anger, resentment and even hatred in extreme situations, is an act of forgiveness in itself.

" As we become more secure in ourselves, things become less important... "

Some people find it easier to accept and forgive, coming from a place of unconditional love, while others may hold a grudge. As we have said, the mind is built to recall things as a way of protection. Even though this doesn't always feel helpful, it does actually keep us alive. Knowing this, the task then is to take charge and rationalise our response. This allows us to find our own place of emotional safety. In many instances, generally no one is at fault, when we change the way we communicate with ourselves we can achieve internal consolation.

When we accept a situation for what is it and spend less time mulling it round and round, then a considerable number of choices arise. We are able to 'see the wood for the trees'. Great things come into our awareness and ones that have far more value than the original issue.

Just to say, in order to accept a situation does not mean that you have to like it or agree with it. Some people say that acceptance makes us vulnerable and like a 'doormat'. It is actually the opposite as you take back the power. By accepting what has happened and dealing with your part in it, then you can be free from mental and emotional blockages. Quite often our own behaviour and that of others is negative and sometimes clearly unacceptable. This still is not an opportunity to hold on to it. By letting go we can become more rational and reasonable. We can choose to accept the other person's ways as just that; bearing in mind no one is perfect. This allows our next move.

Practising and mastering acceptance shifts you into accepting yourself fully as the person you are. Real self-acceptance comes from accepting the things you like about yourself and the things you don't. It comes from allowing yourself to experience thoughts and feelings without denial, self-punishment or rejection. As we have said earlier, negative emotions can be the cause of many illnesses. By learning to accept yourself, your attention can go to working on the self-limiting beliefs that hold you back rather than self-beating.

STEP to CHANGE

Letting go of the past

Letting go of the past

Take a moment to think about your own situation

It is important to free yourself from past experiences to be able to move on. Have a go at writing down all, and I mean ALL, the painful, hurtful situations you are still affected by. Include anything you have regret for or feel a sense of guilt about.

Commit them to paper and, as you read each one back to yourself or even out loud, start to notice that you have the power to let go of these old stories.

Keep repeating this every day for 2 weeks and notice a change in how you feel.

I accept ....happened and
I am willing to let go of ....

I accept ....happened and
I am willing to let go of ....

I accept ....happened and
I am willing to let go of ....

If you have done this on a separate piece of paper, you can destroy the paper - rip it up or burn it (carefully!)

Now think of all the parts of yourself you find difficult to accept. Either say each day or even say while you look in the mirror.

I accept .... about myself

I accept .... about myself

I accept .... about myself

Forgiveness

Our growth starts in the forgiveness process. Accepting that something has happened is only part of letting go. There is also the challenge of forgiveness. This can be for things that have happened, people and ourselves. We will never forget difficult times but being stuck with them is not a good place. These memories can be more like stop signs on your life path, where as learning and letting go are vital to have happiness and fulfilment. We get there at a greater speed too.

"Don't let the speed bumps of life become a stop sign..."

Forgiveness is not easy and can often be more painful than the initial hurt itself. Forgiveness also doesn't mean that we are excusing someone else's, or our own, poor behaviour. When we let go of the hurtful emotions associated with memories of the past, we become peaceful and claim our power back to cope in the future. By holding on, we are draining ourselves and will stay weakened. By freeing ourselves, we are strong and resilient – another mind gym exercise.

Forgiving those involved in old stories of a past relationship or situation helps us grow and focus on new things in the future. When we think of all the things that went wrong and sit in blame, it brings in negativity and the risk is the likelihood of the same behaviours reoccurring.

Self-forgiveness is like reclaiming our freedom from the past and this can often be harder work than forgiving others. It is the one that most people neglect. Through being curious and self-reflective, we find ourselves in a state of forgiveness. We are the only ones who can separate us from other people's drama.

STEP to CHANGE

Forgiveness

Forgiveness

Take a moment to think about your own situation

Learning to forgive ourselves and others is no mean feat. It takes determination and commitment. We need to think about this task like we are at the gym again, building up strength in our mind muscles.

This is an exercise to repeat regularly. It is powerful to write this down, as seeing them visually strengthens the power and helps with the repetitive nature of changing the neutral network.

Recall anyone in your life who you hold a negative emotion or thoughts about. Then write and read out the answers to these statements.

Again, repeat and repeat until you feel
a sense of relief.

Forgiveness of Others

The person I need to forgive is ....
and I forgive you for ....

The person I need to forgive is ....
and I forgive you for ....

The person I need to forgive is ....
and I forgive you for ....

Do this time and time again.

Forgiveness of Self

Then turn the exercise onto yourself, and think about all the things that you blame yourself for and say:

I truly forgive myself for ....

I truly forgive myself for ....

I truly forgive myself for ....

Again, repeat and repeat until you feel a sense of relief.

Expectations

Forgiveness of ourselves or others is much more difficult when we have high expectations, which then causes challenges for us. An expectation is a belief about what should have happened in the past or what should happen in the future. For example, you have an expectation of yourself to stay close with your best friends your whole life. This might not be a reality as your lives might take you in a different direction. We can find ourselves in trouble without realising when we have high expectations of ourselves, others or both. These can often be unrealistic and cause conflict and disappointment. These 'high bars' that we set ourselves are often as a result of limiting beliefs, for example 'I'm not good enough so I need to be perfect' or 'I need to gain my parents approval', so consequently we will be very hard on ourselves.

We need to be more mindful of the problem in judging ourselves (often harshly) when we don't quite achieve as much as we wanted or against what others have said. When we judge ourselves, the behaviour we are unhappy with becomes the focus.

There is a clear link to the high expectations many of us set ourselves with what other people will think. This may be parents, other family members, partners, friends and colleagues. When you think about it most people spend a lot of time worried about what others think of them, which means, the next person is doing the same. They too are worrying about what others think of them. So maybe we could move the focus onto ourselves to make decisions for ourselves. Keep this in mind as it does help to clear some of the self-imposed pressure.

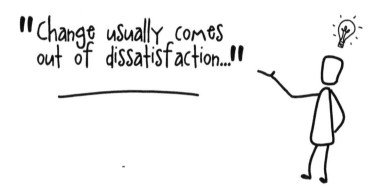

"Change usually comes out of dissatisfaction..."

When we look at some of our behaviours, we can start to separate what is being driven by our own expectation or pressure put on by someone else. It is natural to be concerned about what someone else thinks, although not healthy if it creates negative pressure and unhappiness. We would be crazy to think that we can be liked by everyone or to think that we can make someone think certain things about us. When we are aiming to succeed influenced by someone else's expectation then this can end in misery.

A sure route to unhappiness is when we regularly do things because we think someone else thinks we should, and yet if we asked ourselves 'who said we should', the answer is usually 'no one did'! We put ourselves under so much pressure and can tie ourselves up in knots trying desperately to get it right - but right for whom? Not necessarily ourselves.

When we put too much emphasis on what others will think of us, rather than accepting our own 'true' self - in other words placing disproportionate emphasis on what society and others expect of us and how we 'ought to' act - it can become a 'tyranny of the shoulds'. We feel that we 'should'; 'have to'; 'must'; 'need'; 'ought to' do certain things out of duty, obligation or compulsion or simply because we think others will judge us.

Word of warning, when you feel the pressure of other people's expectation, bear in mind, these are quite probably your own. This is emphasised again in Step 4 – The Power of Language.

STEP to CHANGE

Noticing 'SHOULD' statements

Noticing 'SHOULD' statements

Take some time to think about your own situation

Spend a bit of time reflecting what you think you should do, should have done and shouldn't have. Notice if this is coming from someone else's expectation or your own.

I should ....

....

Who says? ....

I should ....

....

Who says? ....

I should ....

....

Who says? ....

I should have ....

I should have ....

I should have ....

I shouldn't have ....

I shouldn't have ....

I shouldn't have ....

Rescuing others

We have identified that most of us do a lot of things because we think we should although it is good to understand the motivation behind some of our behaviours. The next thing to be mindful of is whether our actions are of a rescuing behaviour. This behaviour can feel like a positive one, because you are considering someone else, looking out for them and generally being nice. The question is at whose expense.

Sometimes the desire to help is very strong and can be problematic. It's interesting to notice what drives us towards pleasing others or doing too much for them. While it can feel like you are being a great partner, friend or family member, it does have a high price to pay. It usually means we are avoiding looking at ourselves. Remember we have talked about the drama triangle and becoming a rescuer for others. For some people, there becomes a constant need to fix or rescue others. When we do this, we are usually not looking after ourselves and the risk is burn-out. It is good to emphasise this again as the behaviour can be linked to guilt and the belief that the rescuer 'should' run around or 'must' tell others what they need to be doing. Rescuers can find themselves making promises to others, and yet need to learn to make and keep promises to themselves.

When we detach ourselves from the need to be the rescuer, the focus is then on us and our own needs. A great metaphor for life is the same as the advice we are given on an airplane - 'Please put on our own oxygen mask before you attempt to help someone else'.

We know now that we need to look after ourselves before we help someone else, we have a new self-awareness, an ability to reflect on our auto responses and work on letting go of our 'stuff' using many different options.

Reframing

Step 3 is called Reframing. This is a powerful approach and we will explore how to look at situations from a different perspective. This creates clarity, helps us to move away from the blame game and allows us to take personal responsibility with ease.

Reframing helps us to be more proficient at stepping back from what has happened in a situation and to consider whether there is a different perspective. When we reframe, it is like looking through a different lens as we identify an alternative viewpoint. This can be done with situations from the past or in the present. We also disrupt the irrational thoughts and initial emotional response, which help us to be more positive in our next steps.

This approach links to a lot of what we have talked about through the book. If we go with the idea that everything usually happens for a reason and that there is something good for us in most situations. Reframing can help us to see good or rational alternatives. A problem is often an opportunity. Reframing helps us to reduce the amount of drama and then move on. Sometimes we can turn even catastrophic events into something positive. For example, there is a huge crash on the motorway and we are going to be late for work.

We can be grateful that it is not us in the crash rather than being stressed and frustrated that we are going to be late. Reframing gives a different perspective, have a go for yourself.

STEP to CHANGE

A different perspective

A different perspective

Take a moment to practise visualising your struggle from a different perspective.

Think of a situation you are currently struggling with:

and then what emotions you have

Now image that you can float or fly up high and then look down on this situation. You can create your own metaphor for this visualisation.

Or you can think of it like this:

1) See your mind as the sky, vast and clear, then the waves of emotion are clouds which will pass. The emotions that we experience are largely fabrications of our mind, and just as they appear, they can drift away too.

Or

2) Imagine a stormy sea with huge breakers. Each wave is bigger than the last. They are about to engulf your boat; your very life hangs in the balance for a few minutes. Then imagine observing the same scene from a high-flying plane. From that perspective, the waves seem to form a delicate, blue-and-white mosaic, barely trembling on the surface of the water. From that height, in the silence, you feel calm and relaxed.

What can you notice about your own situation from a different perspective?

Values

How we view and experience our world through the current 'frame' is very much influenced by our values. Our values are a key driver of happiness and fulfilment in life. Values, such as trust, love, and integrity act as an internal guidance system and when all is well these are at the heart of every major decision we make, even if we are not aware that this is happening. They are unique to each of us and there is no right and wrong about them. They are integral and what is an important value to one, isn't necessarily for another. Although we all share values as many of them make the human world function, we often attach our own meaning to them.

Our values are important because they help us to grow and develop. They help us to create the future we want to experience. We all make hundreds of decisions every day. Every decision we make and everything we say and do reflects our values and beliefs. When we use our values to make decisions, we make a deliberate choice to focus on what is important to us.

When we make choices that fulfil our values, we are more likely to feel content and satisfied. For example, when you have a value around making a difference and your work allows you to fulfil this value, then you will see your work as satisfying.

Something that is usually out of our awareness is when some of our unhappiness comes from not living by these values. If we commit any time or energy to something that neglects or violates our core values, we start to feel resentment and frustration. When we are not honouring our values in our choices, there will be a nagging within that something is missing or wrong in our life.

For example, if you are in a position where honesty is important to you and you work in an environment where there is poor communication, and you feel out the loop, then this situation will cause you a problem.

In many situations when you feel angry, frustrated or stuck, there is a high chance that you are not living through your values. You are likely to be ignoring or neglecting what is important to you or allowing your values to be violated. Another example, you have an uneasy feeling about a manager and this is affecting your commitment to your job. Ordinarily, you are a person who goes the extra mile and has a lot of pride in your achievements. You feel rubbish because you are not fulfilling your values of being hardworking and allowing the attitude or behaviour of the manager to affect you. In these types of situations, you need to focus on what is happening within you and you know now not to get fixated on the behaviour of others. This could be one of those lessons you very much need, and action is required.

STEP to CHANGE

Your values

Your values

Take a moment to think about your own situation.

This exercise will help bring your values to life. Firstly, pick a context or subject you would like to explore, such as relationships, work, health or life in general.

List everything that pops into your mind. Keep asking yourself the same question until you come up with a huge list of your values.

Examples are: trust, love, honesty, loyalty, friendship, making a difference, money, or success at work.

Now spend some time reflecting on these and check to see if you are living through your values. In other words, are your current choices in life allowing your values to be fulfilled. If you notice that some are not, this could be why there is discord in your life and you need to think about making changes.

Then ask yourself:

In the context of ....
....
....
(relationships, work, health), what is important to me?

Do you fulfilled them?

Do you neglect them?

Are they violated?

Change your focus

Our goal is to be able to focus on what we want. This might just be having a positive mental attitude, which although sounds simple is an important achievement to master. Positive people have a clear mindset that is focused on success, self-belief, deserving and happiness to name but a few.

As you become more aware of your thoughts and internal world, then less will be happening in autopilot, and therefore you will feel more positive. From here, you have an opportunity to change how you think and talk which ultimately changes the outcome.

It is common to hear people talking about what they want in the negative. Often, we are focused on the fear of something happening which ultimately means a negative focus. A couple of examples could be if you fear someone leaving you; losing your job; worry about not finding a job; then you are spending a lot of time and energy focusing on the what you don't want. Over time, these thought patterns result in you starting to believe what you fear and that you only deserve disappointment. This can lead to destructive thinking. We then start to feel disheartened and, worst still, sabotage anything that is good. When we live in fear of something bad happening, guess what, that bad something usually happens.

Whilst focusing on the worst-case scenario you raise the risk of habit thinking and talking about what you don't want rather than what you do want. For example, 'I don't want to feel stressed', 'I don't want to be insecure', 'I don't want to be fat' and so the list goes on. Surprisingly enough, when you do this you are likely to get what you don't want. You end up feeling stressed, worried etc.

Later in this chapter, we will discuss further how the subconscious mind is not able to process the word 'don't'. It is so important to change this and embed the positive in your language, both to yourself and others. For now, though, the task is to get clear on what you want in your future and bring this to life.

Visualisation

Science has now been able to provide us with an explanation of how our brain prefers images. The human capacity for imagination not only shapes our minds but also weaves the fabric of reality itself. Being able to get what we want is amplified when we are able to visualise it. Successful people can visualise themselves being successful and see themselves already there.

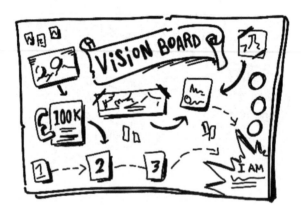

One very powerful tool is creating a vision board which is a visualisation of all that you want in life. The process of making one encourages your focus in the right direction, plus is also fun and inspirational. Vision boards are a modern manifestation tool combining concepts taken from creative hobbies like scrapbooking with motivational mind-mapping techniques. It's like your very own treasure map.

The idea behind this is that when you surround yourself with images of who you want to become, what you want to have, where you want to live, or where you want to go, like on holiday, your focus changes to match those images and those desires.

A vision board is quite literally a collage of pictures, phrases, poems and quotes visually representing what you would like to experience more of in your life.

STEP to CHANGE

Create your own VISION BOARD

Create your own VISION BOARD

Let's get creative here, start to collect images, pictures, quotes, photos which will make up your very own vision board. Once you have collected your images, get an A3 Foam Board or a large piece of paper and enjoy creating your vision of the best version of yourself and your life. This is a powerful technique and certainly one to take your time with.

It would be fabulous to share your finished board on 2minds Facebook page.

VISION BOARD TO DO ....

☑ Scissors & Glue...
☑ BREW
☑ A3 Foam Board !
☑ Magazines
☑ Photos & Affirmations!

333

Challenging your limiting beliefs

We have explored limiting beliefs and have acknowledged how they can hold us back. By naming our limiting beliefs, taking an honest position and being aware of them, we have already taken a huge step towards changing them. Along with reframing your thoughts and assumptions about your life.

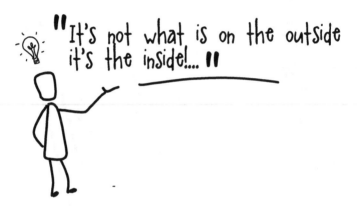

"It's not what is on the outside it's the inside!...."

In order to prevent false beliefs from taking control of your life, the gremlin in your mind needs to be carefully managed. It is common to get frustrated and angry with yourself. However, dealing with the loud voice that keeps shouting 'Who do you think you are?', 'You couldn't possibly do that!' or 'What would people think if you did that?' needs to be treated gently, though challenged ultimately. You must be gentle as the mind is trying to protect you so getting angry with yourself doesn't help.

We need to start to push those self-limiting boundaries and move forward. By being aware, this is both good to make changes although also scary. We might notice that we often have a finger permanently over the destruct button, putting ourselves down or being hard on ourselves or sabotaging anything that resembles good. We need to start to notice the moment we become hard on ourselves for our reaction or behaviours.

The act of being kind is a good place to start, regardless of the deep-rooted thinking. Thoughts are actually just thoughts. They don't have to be true, nor do we need to take action on them.

STEP to CHANGE

Challenging your own beliefs

Challenging your own beliefs

Take a moment to think about your own situation

Bring any negative beliefs and thoughts about yourself, use the answers from the previous exercises and let's take a different approach to dealing with it rather than letting it take over and drag you down.

Following these steps and questions will help you manage those negative beliefs.

Firstly, thank yourself for bringing this thought and belief to your attention. Keep asking yourself these questions:

Is this belief actually true? e.g. Am I truly not good enough or am I truly unlovable?

Do I have any real evidence that supports it? What has actually happened?

Does it resemble old stories? Think about how?

Is this just someone else's view? Does this need to define you?

By starting to accept what has really happened, not what our limiting beliefs will have us believe, we are in a better position to make great changes. By noticing what we are doing to ourselves and acknowledging that blaming someone else doesn't get us anywhere, we are finally in a position to move forward. A situation is very rarely what we thought it was. Our limiting beliefs are incredibly powerful and will run us a merry dance given half the chance. This can quite simply start with a trigger to a thought or a connection to an old story and we feel dreadful in that moment.

With all these strategies and tools to practice, you can start to change your reality, take back your power and lead the life you want. It is time to concentrate on the last step in this book Step 4 - how you communicate with yourself and others.

The power of language

Step 4 is communication and language: our own internal voice and how we communicate to others. This fundamentally is a massive topic as everything is about how we communicate. Everything we have covered so far is a form of communication. As we talk to ourselves and others, we are listening, interpreting and responding. It can be like a dance. As communication is probably at the root of all challenges, we will break down some aspects so that you can identify where change is necessary. How we communicate has a huge impact on the outcome in any situation.

Words

Language is the most powerful tool we have and yet can cause us so many challenges. Wars have been started, deals have been lost and relationships destroyed over words.

In his book, Change One Word at a Time, David Firth, author, consultant and speaker, reports that we speak 16,000 words a day. There are ways of speaking that produce action and change and there are ways of speaking that don't. This can produce happiness and progress or negativity and unhappiness. A little like our thoughts, how many of our words are good, productive ones?

For most of us, our words are spoken without consciousness. We rarely stop to think about what we are saying. Our thoughts, opinions, judgements and beliefs roll off our tongues without a care for the damage or the benefits they can produce. While we have acknowledged that the emotional response is always the first one for the mind, it doesn't necessarily mean it is the right one to follow. The old saying 'bite your tongue' springs to mind! We often end up saying things that rationally we don't mean. Also remember the subconscious mind takes everything literally, so it believes all thoughts and words and creates a response accordingly. For this reason, gossip and judgement become like poison into our bodies. It robs us of a clear mind. We often judge others when we feel unhappy or angry, which then fuels our own systems with negativity and we are caught in a vicious circle. Our negative self-talk is probably at large.

Unhelpful language

There are many ways that we can change the way we talk and what language we use. There are a few quick wins to challenge negativity and these will affect what happens next. Let's have a look at a few.

- ### *The tyranny of should*

We have already mentioned the tyranny of should earlier, although it needs reiterating in this chapter.

How many times a day do you hear yourself saying 'I should ....'?

We get into trouble with using 'should' when it takes the form of these automatic thoughts. The idea of choice moves us closer to doing something. A 'should' can stem from guilt, a choice leads to action. 'I should decorate my house', 'I should sort out my life'. While we do need to do things in life to get on, we certainly are not obliged to act on all our thoughts. If we choose to do something out of choice then this will (to some degree, at least) change the outcome for the better. When we do 'should' things, these are linked to pressure, guilt or other people. This is likely to make us miserable and comes back to doing things that are wrong for us.

Equally, words like 'ought' and 'must' all relate to demands and high expectations, and link to behaviours we have explored like people pleasing, rescuer and victim position thinking. These words drive us to behave through the expectations of others, not particularly ourselves.

A quick release from this trap is to watch out for how often we say, 'I should do X and Y', and then ask yourself 'Who actually says you should?' More often than not, it is completely our own self-imposed pressure which in itself becomes a reframe and potentially lets go of the guilt.

- **Don't**

As mentioned before we want to work towards focusing on what we want rather than what we don't. Remember the human mind is powerful and creative and yet it's as if it has a few flaws in its functioning. One of these is that the subconscious mind is unable to process the word 'don't'.

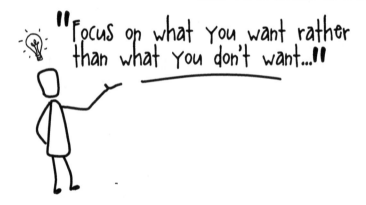

"Focus on what you want rather than what you don't want..."

So when we think or say, 'I don't want to be upset', 'I don't want to be stressed or anxious', 'I don't want to feel insecure', 'I don't want to cry', 'I don't want to be with a person like that again', our subconscious mind is unable to process the simple word 'don't' and actually hears a direct instruction to do exactly what is not wanted. Think of a sign which reads 'Don't go on the grass', there is a part of us that wants to go on the grass. It is only our conscious mind which knows this means 'stay off the grass'!

Small children demonstrate this perfectly because they live in their subconscious world. When you say to a small child, 'Don't touch the TV', 'Don't spill your drink' or 'Don't run on the road', the child just seems to do exactly what you have just asked them not to do. What the child is actually hearing is a direct instruction – touch the TV, spill your drink and could frighteningly run on the road. These instructions can be very confusing to children and can shape us as adults, possibly leading to the creation of limiting beliefs and confusion in terms of emotional growth.

Adult subconscious minds are no different from the child in this context. The difference is our conscious, rational mind knows what is meant, although it is the subconscious mind that creates the reality for us. So, going back to the examples before, saying 'Come away from the TV', 'Put your cup on the table', and 'Stay on the pavement' will get a completely different response. Try it; it is amazing to see the difference.

For you, it is vital that you say what you want also. For if you find yourself saying 'I don't want to be stressed', then what exactly is it that you do want? Do you want to be calm? Do you want to be confident? This language change makes an enormous amount of difference to how the subconscious mind processes and then on what happens as a result. Remember what you focus on becomes your reality.

- **But**

Another word used frequently is the little, yet powerful word 'but'. Some people use it habitually and, without realising it are pointing out the negative aspects of a situation. Do you realise that when the word 'but' is used, it negates anything that has been said immediately prior? For example, 'I have had a lovely day, but the weather was rubbish'. The 'but' takes the focus from the lovely day. We all do this far too often, and the trick is to change our language and use the word 'and' in its place. Going back to the example, 'I have had a lovely day, and the weather was rubbish'.

The little word 'but' is also a big avoider. It peppers our language with excuses why we don't do things or take action. It also gives a free rein to any limiting thoughts and beliefs to hold us back.

For example; 'I'm normal weight but my arms are fat', 'I'm active but I really should do more exercise', 'I play the piano but I'm not very good', 'I'm really good at my job but I will never get a promotion, 'I'd like to travel more but I can't leave my mother on her own', 'I'm miserable in this relationship but I'm scared to leave'.

STEP to CHANGE

Your language

Your language

Take a moment to think about your own situation

Spend the next few days noticing your own language and that of others. See if you can spot the use of these little words. Remember, being aware is the first place to start.

How many times do you say:

'I should…. ,'I must …..' I shouldn't… but ………………………

Are you focused on what you don't want rather than what you do want?

I don't want to ....

I don't want to ....

I don't want to ....

Looking at the above statements, think about what you want to happen instead.

What do you want to happen

I want to ....

I want to ....

I want to ....

Heated conversations

All that we have explored so far helps us with our own self-talk as well as with our interactions with others. Many conversations with others so easily involve some misunderstanding, it is just the way we are. What is difficult is when it turns into conflict. Even normal interactions may involve faulty communication, the ones with conflict often escalate. Sometimes this can lead to an even worse problem than in the first place. The higher the level of conflict, the costlier misunderstandings may be. We have all been in situations where our communication has made the difference.

"Unkindness is lack of understanding"

Given our tendency to hear what we expect to hear or what we interpret, it is very easy for people in conflict to misunderstand each other. In these circumstances, communication is likely to be strained, and the potential for misperceptions and misunderstandings is high.

When we go into these high emotional states, each person is not able to hear the other one clearly. This is because both are too busy getting their point across and that point is often irrational. Both are in drama with little thought of what is being said. We can be very out of character. We have all been there and yet these kinds of discussions, or arguments, clearly don't get us anywhere. It takes a brave person to step away from this kind of argument.

When emotions are high, everything seems clouded, particularly our explanations and interpretations. So often when our conversation is reflected back to us, we find ourselves responding with 'I didn't mean it like that'. There are many occasions when words are interpreted as nothing like they were intended. This misinterpretation is even worse with present day electronic communication (such as texts) missing core components of communication such as eye contact, facial expression and particularly tone.

In communication, we can be surprised and frustrated by the responses we get. In calmer situations, a misunderstanding may simply be rectified with a re-explanation or repeated to be heard properly. When it truly doesn't work is when it has triggered off a heated conversation, causing disarray. The disagreement has resulted in a need to justify or defend ourselves. It is ok to have our own view and interpretation, although when we expect someone to understand us, this can cause challenges. While we know this, we also need to keep in mind that those limiting beliefs are often being fired up and causing havoc to thoughts and feelings. Another reason people are not good at communicating is because they don't listen! People are often too focused on their own internal dialogue and are literally formulating their answer rather than listening.

"Listen to understand, not to respond...!"

During this time, we start to listen to our own thoughts and not to the other person. The risk here is misinterpretation or simply jumping in too early. Regularly we speak without thought and end up in all sorts of trouble! We know that based on a few words, or a few sentences, we often create a perspective on something or someone, which may be inaccurate because we didn't take the time to listen. It is so obvious that every situation has two sides to it although we often forget this, particularly when in drama.

We have been blessed with the gift of communication, the gift to express our feelings, emotions, ideas or plans with words. Speaking and listening in a balanced way are imperative in our world.

We often keep those negative thoughts and associated emotions alive after a heated conversation. This is only hurting us and will affect further conversations. We will continue to try to get our point across, all the wrong words come out heavily loaded with emotions. There is often a lot of wasted energy, and time, and we can be left feeling isolated and frustrated.

How we speak to each other determines the quality of our relationship or how we view ourselves. It is key to be able to notice the difference between words of inclusion rather than separation; words of acceptance rather than rejection; words of tolerance rather than prejudice. Our words put out an energy or message that creates a reaction.

Let's pause now and do some self reflection. It is good to think about what you have learned about yourself. Here are some questions to help you with this task:

STEP to CHANGE

Self-reflection

Self-reflection

Take a moment to think about your own situation

Reflect on everything that you have learned about yourself?

What have you learnt about yourself?

What do you need to do more of?

What do you need to do differently?

What do you need to less of?

What do you need to stop doing all together?

Using criticism

We have explored the common place criticism takes in our lives, whether that is to ourselves or others. Negative comments from others make us doubt and question ourselves and we feel like we are being attacked. What we also know now to be true is that they could trigger and 'play' to any limiting beliefs lurking within us, which makes us feel twice as bad.

We need to be able to separate the nasty comments from others which are usually said in rage or revenge. Many are not true, more likely their own reflection and therefore unhelpful. However, some and often the harshest comments can be a vital part for our development. They may be seeing something that we can't see or are not ready to admit about ourselves. When we get out of drama, we can often reflect that we were being difficult, unreasonable or over-sensitive, which is exactly what the other person was saying. This route for learning is probably one of the hardest ways to accept and yet can be very powerful.

Learning and changing relies in a large part on recognising then analysing and addressing our challenges. Other people can often help highlight negative behaviours which can be difficult to admit initially, although become a gift to appreciate in the long run. The biggest benefit of 'feedback' is it reveals something that may be in our blind spot or not in our awareness yet. It's important to separate the unhelpful opinions and unhelpful criticism first. Then look for the gems for ourselves.

We need to be ready and open to hear this, accept it and take action. There may be real evidence or relevance to their comments or they can see something deep and hidden. Sometimes there are behaviours, feelings or traits that we would love to ignore! We have a choice to hear them as negative criticism or we could see them as areas of development. We can see both our dark side and good side through others.

We need to be brave to admit our flaws and sometimes these are only obvious through viewing our own behaviour alongside someone else. As we get to know someone else, we are often learning more about ourselves through their different ways of being. The realisation pushes us to change, even though at the time it feels awful and a direct criticism.

We also need to bear in mind that very often other people's observations, comments and criticism are often more about them than us. We are all each other's mirrors and we often see in others what we witness in ourselves. The behaviours we are happy with go unnoticed although often the ones we don't like are the ones we criticise others for. This is also happening for the person criticising you. The behaviour to criticise gives a distraction from looking at ourselves. This concept suggests that both parties, if they are aware and open to development, are showing up in each other and there are opportunities for learning.

Giving positive feedback

We can't deny that there is so much power in words and thoughts. When you uplift someone with your words, notice how much better you feel in yourself. As you know, the subconscious mind takes everything personally, so when you have spoken positively about or to someone else, you will take this internally and make it true for you. Then you feel good too and this is another mind gym exercise which builds resilience and self-worth. The great thing about this is you can do it anytime, anywhere and you are building yourself up, along with the other person. We leave a lasting impression because of the feelings both parties have.

The challenge is to keep this in mind as it is just as true when we are talking negatively about someone else. The mind believes what you are saying is about you and so you don't feel as good. Be careful what you say and think about someone else, as it is very likely to be as much about you and your mind will take it personally.

Giving constructive feedback

As we have established having others understand us and be able to interpret us safely is probably one of the hardest things to master. Being able to make a comment or give another feedback that is useful and meaningful to them is difficult. We now understand that we will each interpret everything differently based on our previous experiences. We so often see things differently and yet we see ourselves in each other too. It is such a puzzle at times.

As we all know giving unhelpful feedback in the form of criticism just creates conflict and defensiveness. However, as we have explored earlier, we are often seeing things in others that are helpful to another, they just haven't realised it yet. A vital component which makes all the difference is how it is said. The best way to give someone feedback is to ensure that it is based on evidence, on something tangible that has been seen or heard. That way the other person can recognise what you are referring too.

More commonly feedback is given using the impact on us or the emotional response to a situation which then causes issues. If someone says, 'you made me feel angry when you didn't call me', the other person is likely to hear the emotion and naturally will try and defend this. A better response would be 'when I didn't hear from you, I felt upset'.

As with the example above, another common response to other people's behaviours is that we often think that someone has made us feel hurt or angry. No one actually has this power over another. You are feeling angry in response to something that they have done rather than them controlling your emotions. This needs to be considered when feedback is given, as this again isn't helpful to another. If you can't provide some evidence in the feedback, then it isn't feedback for the other person. In these situations where there is no actual evidence, it is as we have explored through this book, your own internal world that has been triggered causing you some discomfort. This could be one of those gems that we are looking out for. A potential for growth within you rather than blaming the other person for your emotional response.

Recognising your worth

Our language has so much power and can change the reality. When we need to build up our self-confidence and self-worth, there are some words and phrases that are vital. The words in a statement 'I am ....' can change how we see ourselves and how we feel about ourselves. These are called affirmations. We have been conditioned to believe that who we are is ordinary, that who we are is what we have, what we do, what people think of us and what we own. None of this is who we really are. We are who we believe we are, so let's make sure the thinking is right.

Because the subconscious mind believes everything you say or think, then the great news about this next exercise is you can choose words that describe how you want to be. For example, I am confident can be something you are working towards although repeating the 'I am ....' like a mantra is powerful and a clear instruction to the subconscious mind.

STEP to CHANGE

Your affirmations

Your affirmations

Take a moment to think about your own situation

Write down 5 positive, 'I am' statements or affirmations.

Saying them to yourself each day, out loud if possible, and a number of times a day, is even better.

For example; I am lovable, I am creative or I am secure.

I am ....

I am ....

I am ....

I am ....

I am ....

Expressing gratitude

When we are making a conscious effort to change negative beliefs and become a stronger, happier person our internal world starts moving in different directions. We focus on new ideas, opportunities and find solutions to challenges.

Being grateful and acknowledging who, what and how you are is vital for a strong mind. This is yet another exercise at the mind gym. When we spend some time, ideally each day, thinking about what we are grateful for and acknowledging any achievements, big or small, we empower ourselves. We become happier, and more resilient. This seems so simple and yet when asked most people admit to not doing it.

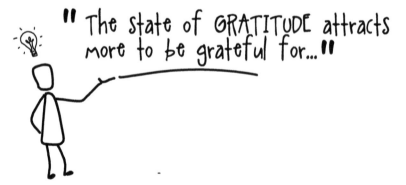

"The state of GRATITUDE attracts more to be grateful for..."

One reason we are not great at acknowledging what we have or have achieved is because we are so busy chasing after the next thing. We want or find ourselves focused on what we haven't done or haven't got and then forget to enjoy the present moment. Most adults are guilty of this. We forget to be happy now, be fulfilled in the moment because we have already moved onto the 'next' and put our happiness dependent on something else.

People say things like 'Oh, I will be happy when I will get this and that', 'when I will get there', 'when I will do this and that'...when those things do happen, they go on to planning the next thing and the next thing, forgetting to enjoy the things they achieved or got so far. Don't let that be you.

Make this a daily activity for a greater impact. Spend time each day noticing what you are grateful for. This can be anything and everything. The attitude of gratitude creates more of the same and an abundance of great things into your life.

Setting your intention

Throughout this book and journey together, we have been exploring ideas and options to build up self-esteem, self-worth and confidence. Another, and vital one, is being clear on where you are going and what you are doing. Equally you can set your intention for how you want to feel.

A working definition for intention is 'to have in mind a purpose or plan, to direct the mind, to aim'. Lacking intention means there is a risk that we usually stray without direction and are unhappy. When we have a clear direction, it is like all the internal and external forces can align to make even the most impossible, possible. Use intentions to transform the conversation around dreams from fear and doubt to hope and possibility, followed by action and results.

We all need some direction and a sense of purpose in life. This naturally builds happiness and fulfilment. The mind doesn't like uncertainty and ambiguity. We firstly need to know where we are, so we can design the appropriate plan for getting to where we want to be. The challenge is our attitude to both our hopes and our 'reality'. When we are stuck, we think that the current reality is permanent or that we feel like we are in a revolving door. It is important to be realistic although having no plan is the road block.

We know that our subconscious minds are listening and reacting to all our thoughts and spoken words. We need to think and speak with intention and with integrity. Remember, we construct our reality, and this is a game changer. Use positive words of encouragement, appreciation, love, acceptance, possibility and vision and there will be movement. This may feel alien at first although the power is in this intention.

STEP to CHANGE

Setting your intentions

Setting your intentions

Take a moment to think about your own situation.

By setting an intention, we make it clear to ourselves and others that we are serious about our dreams.

Get clear about something you want (a goal) and write it down (you may want to return to the vision board you designed in the re-framing section)

Create some steps to achieving it

Who can you share your goal with as an accountability?

What can you do today to demonstrate your commitment?

Celebrate that you have taken a step and think about the next step.

Changing your self-talk

We have already explored the negative voices inside our minds. We have also established that we can't stop thoughts. They will always be there and often like a running a commentary on our moment-by-moment experiences, the quality of our past decisions, mistakes we could have avoided, and what we *should* have done differently. These voices can be mean and make a bad situation infinitely worse. They appear automatic, fear-based 'rules for living' that can act like inner bullies, keeping us stuck in the same old cycles and hampering our spontaneous enjoyment of life. Our ability to live and love freely.

While the deep-rooted origin of this voice can be harder to change, there is no doubt that there is a lot we can do to minimise the impact. We certainly don't have to pay attention or respond to all our thoughts. As the mind believes everything literally, then we can be playful and reduce the negative voice. By giving the mind an instruction of what we want to happen to the comments then we can change the impact. We can literally say THANKS BUT NO THANKS or another idea is saying 'Ah there you are again negative voice, NO THANKS'!

As we said at the beginning of this journey, the subconscious mind loves to be playful, just like a young child, and so these approaches can improve the situation. It seems quite a crazy approach as an adult, although it gives you an idea how powerful the mind is. You can choose to listen to this voice or not – it is your choice.

We can play a little with the inner voice too. We can try turning down the volume of the punishing, judgemental, negative voice, telling us we are no good or not adequate. This will then have less power. We can change the voice to a funny, squeaky voice for a bit of fun or the voice of a character. Sometimes saying your thoughts out loud in this voice has a great result! As adults we take ourselves very seriously and this is often linked to the power of the negativity. When we can smile or even laugh at the negative voice, the impact is less.

These changes then help you to switch your attention to something else and you can then use any of the positive beliefs, affirmations and ideas that you have been developing throughout this book. As with any ideas, they can be personalised so that you find what works best for you.

When we are challenging negative self-talk, it is a constant and repetitive task. It takes effort and persistence to break and create a habit although well worth it.

Take responsibility for your own feelings

We have spent time acknowledging that it is a normal human trait to take what other people say personally. We now know that we all interpret through our own lens and this can leave us feeling criticised or even violated. We then are likely to blame the other person or situation for our feelings. It is interesting that we never 'blame' someone for making us feel happy and yet do it instantly in a negative situation.

It's good to remember that the first response to most things is an emotional one. Each of us will respond differently to whatever is happening. Some find certain things upsetting or create anger which others can feel ok about. Equally what makes us happy and content is different. What is interesting is that we can be even surprised by our response.

The advantages of taking responsibility for our responses means that we move away from the blaming of others, which is what gets us stuck and miserable. As hard as it is, we need to get to a place of taking responsibility for our own feelings. This is a must because the reality is that no one else is powerful enough to make someone else feel anything. People regularly say 'he or she makes me feel.......' although this is not true. No other person can make us feel anything unless we allow them. We all have a choice and by blaming the other person we are actually giving our power away.

When we think about feeling good with someone else, we are still choosing to feel happy or smile because of what the other person has done, or the situation has offered. Not because the other person has any power over our emotions. It is us that are allowing the feeling of happiness or contentment.

We are all influenced by what we see and hear. This is a fact; however, we do have a choice as to how we feel. For example, if you just consider these words slowly – sunshine, holiday, laughing, friendship, and celebration – allow yourself to respond as you read them and now notice how did you feel reading those words? Probably a warm, happy feeling, albeit mild as it was just a few words in a book. The reality is the words themselves didn't alter your feelings, it was you who associated the words from information within and chose to feel happy or good whist reading the words.

The same applies for negative responses. We still have the power in what happens. We will obviously have a reaction, although the mistake is when we believe that the other person created the reaction in you.

All of us know people in our lives who drive us crazy. We may have spent countless hours reliving the moments when this person was unfair, unappreciative, or inconsiderate to us. Obviously, the best course of action is to not let them get us angry or not allow ourselves to feel anger towards them. It can be a challenge although a worthwhile one. Getting angry does not improve the situation. We may need to vent for a short while, although life is too short to waste time and energy on feeling bad.

An example is when someone hoots a horn at your driving, or drives to closely. They almost want you to react, although the strongest response is to not be affected at all. The minute you allow this stranger to affect you by getting mad, they have the control over your emotions rather than taking charge of yourself. People can spend hours feeling angry or upset about someone else's behaviour. This behaviour is often based on their perception of the situation which often does not mirror the others.

Keep in mind, we use far more energy being annoyed and angry with someone else or ourselves than the more positive emotions. Remember, our subconscious mind can't tell the difference between ourselves and someone else. This means that our mind will feel the emotion within, regardless of the detail and story. We are often only angry with ourselves, unconsciously, for letting ourselves be affected and yet we have the control in the first place.

Most people we meet will have an influence on us, whether that is good or not, mild or major. We will be influencing them too. We grow and change all the time. Every experience each day can shape us. In many situations, change is good, although people cope and manage change differently. Some people find changing their ways a real stretch. Sometimes new people in your life can expose you to new and exciting adventures, ways of thinking and being, which is all perfect. This is easy to embrace, although remember that challenging parts of us can be revealed through others and these are likely to be the best lessons available.

"Putting Yourself first is an act of SELF LOVE..."

Follow your own path

A natural goal for all of us is to be happy in life. When we take full responsibility for ourselves then we have the control and the right ingredients to actually make that happen. When you are free to decide your own path, and focus on what you really want and deserve, then a momentum is there. Although we want to be supported by key people in life, the real difference comes from following your own path. The reward is you will feel happier, more content and fulfilled.

While you can value your true supporters, it is not safe to think that someone else, or possessions, can make you happy or content. When you rely on others to make you happy you are sitting in a dangerous territory. Be mindful of your own internal world and check that you can reassure and love yourself.

The goal is to feel you are choosing what to do which then makes you feel happy and content. You want to feel good in your own skin, rather than rely on any other person for that. When you can create self-love and are capable of self-nurture then this supports you to achieve contentment. The other additional benefit of getting this right is that you are more likely to attract the right kind of people into your life.

Before we come to the end of this journey together, push your comfort zone and get thinking about what you have always wanted to do. There are some questions in the exercise which might help you to pick your activity. Working through what you need more of or less of is a good way to get there.

Go on, think really deeply about this exercise and ensure you create the life you've always wanted.

STEP to CHANGE

Ask yourself

Ask yourself

Take a moment to think about your own situation.

'What have I always wanted to do?'

'What do I need more of in my life?'

'What do I need less of in my life?'

With the answers to these questions, research a new activity that will light you up and make it happen! Try something new or something that you have wished you had returned too, as long as it pushes your comfort zone a little.

Then think 'What do I need to do to start this rolling?'

Have fun and notice how good you feel when you take action and do something just for yourself.

CHAPTER SIX

The Right Path

The right path

Life is a journey, one that continually changes and is never static. Some stages seem easier and others are more of a challenge. The key is to acknowledge where you are, what got you here and to understand that you can create your life as you want it to be. Even if you are not clear about how all this will happen, just know that your new place is to wonder and become curious about the future, even if it feels a little scary; being out of your comfort zone is good!

It is time now to find your way to unlock your true self and realise your potential. This journey with me, I hope, has started the process of you ironing out the real issues with the 'stuff' which you make up in your head. Many of us seem to get sucked into what 'should' happen and subsequently miss the real opportunities and situations that are right for us. We create behaviours which are destructive, damaging and lead us to feel unhappy and dissatisfied with life. These habits and behaviours become our protector, so we may find ourselves struggling to let them go.

By acknowledging your own deep feelings, beliefs, and barriers you understand 'where you are now'. Then you can think about what you want and work out how you are going to get there. Certainly, remember that things don't have to be like they have always been. We change constantly along the way and this can mean that a situation or relationship which used to work now doesn't. When we learn how it all works, then miracles start to happen.

Life provides wake up calls at significant turning points: marriage, divorce, becoming a parent, recovery, moving, meeting someone new, starting work or getting a new job, an empty nest, retiring, experiencing loss or trauma or working in a dead-end job. While these can be challenging, the hardest situations give us the best lessons. This valuable learning is a big step to creating the right path for you because you are taking responsibility and action rather than avoiding.

My intention for this book is to speak to as many people, far and wide. To pass on encouragement, to motivate and to guide you in whatever direction is best. It is to inspire you not to give up, not to just accept how it has always been and, most importantly, to notice how much more you can achieve.

I want you to know that you are not alone on this journey of life with the ups and downs.

It is important to remember that life is a gift. It is the most precious thing available to us and yet we don't always make it the best we can. This book has presented a general outline of some common challenges and how we can discover the most valuable lessons. It must be said that there is always the easy route, often within our comfort zone, although this may not always be the fulfilling one. We can spend time ignoring our instincts and not living our truth, or we can be courageous and take a different route. The approaches and exercises in this book will ultimately create growth and happiness.

As you journey along your path of self-discovery, remember everything really does happen for a reason and this extends even to having a horrible boss, family conflict, a controlling boyfriend or an unusually challenging friendship. When we are able to take that step back and look at the situation from another's perspective rather than jump to blame, we can see when we are doing too much of one thing or not enough of something else. When we become self-aware, we can sit with any discomfort, notice how it has made us feel and, from here, new insights come. We can then take action, take a new approach and, in some cases, even a new direction.

Just as we all have a unique finger print, we need to remember that we are all different in the way we think and behave. There are big variations in how we are affected by situations. When we become aware of our own way of thinking, being and behaving, then we are more able to see our differences, and this helps enormously in relationships and communication.

We now understand why many of our negative behaviours are created and it is important to know that it is these that hold us back the most. It is us, and us alone, that have the greatest power and impact on our own reality, which means it is us that stops ourselves, not others. We seem to choose to suffer or to challenge ourselves well before we realise that there can be another, easier way.

We have looked at the problems which we learn and mirror from others and how our past is very likely to limit us. We have looked at what happens when people keep hold of old unhelpful stories. We know the impact of self beliefs, 'I am not good enough' or 'I am not loved', and then how our minds will seek out evidence to back this up. These negative beliefs hold us back, can create a 'stuck' feeling and then life is not how we want it to be. It is the voice in our own heads. We often end up misinterpreting other's behaviours or words, imagining they are against us. Once we have become aware of our own patterns, then we can let go or challenge our own negativity from within.

Change is undoubtedly difficult. The mind can resist change and make it a challenge. It can be a bumpy ride, but change is possible. We need to find inner strength and be courageous. We need to be mindful there is the choice to go for the easy option and keep hitting the snooze button. This is often because we are not ready to address the real issue. There needs to be a decision to take action and a step towards the true path.

By noticing what you are thinking and doing, you have a greater chance of making changes. By challenging your thoughts, you will stop the repeated thread and move towards what you want. Being aware is the greatest start of all. Everything that has happened did so for a reason; you have been successful every step of the way when you can take the lessons from your experiences. It is these lessons that are valuable and will reshape the future.

New lens

Now that you can look at yourself and your life through a new lens, you are able to self-reflect, take responsibility, challenge negative thoughts and then you will start to move forward. Once you increase self-awareness and notice what you are doing, you are better equipped to see your own behaviours, as well as those of others. Remember the drama triangle – you will be able to step back and consider the situation from a different perspective. Most importantly, it will give you an insight into how you can unlock your true potential. Once you know and believe you have the power and resources within you, then your new journey begins.

"Is it time to make the choice to change?...."

I hope that you now have more courage to know and be your true self, to recognise what is good for you and to give yourself permission to do it your way. This doesn't mean you need to become selfish or hard faced; just look to increase your self-worth. Know that you don't need to prove yourself to anyone who doesn't understand you, and be happy and content.

When you find yourself conforming to what everyone else expects you to do, going along with things because you should or think that it would be selfish to follow your heart's desire, you can now know that this thinking stops your true path revealing itself. If we all allowed or dared ourselves to follow our heart and dreams, the right situations arise. We would be happy in the right jobs; we would be with the right person and be doing more of the other things that make us 'tick'! You need to be clear on what you want, ensure that your beliefs are aligned to this and go with the learning, even though it may be challenging.

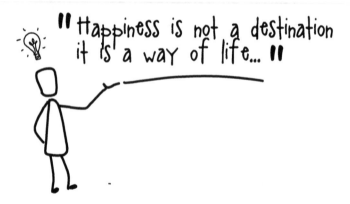

Just remember there is no ending when it comes to happiness, it is a continual journey to joy and fulfilment. Who usually stops you getting what you want? Yep, you are right, YOU!

A little word of warning, when you start to make changes for yourself, or start being a little more assertive with yourself, there can be a 'fall out'. Some will love the 'new' you, for others it can cause some problems initially. If you have been a certain way for most of your life, people have known you like that and a change in your reactions or behaviours can cause issues. There can be a feeling of loss around friendships and/or relationships and family members when you step out and be your true self. Some won't like it and there can be consequences. Some people may even go from your life. There is an old saying: people come into your life for a reason or season. When we make changes, not everyone is able to come along.

The Real You

It is time now to get to know yourself, give yourself permission to be the real you and be on your right path. When you have understood what is holding you back and you have acknowledged guilt, despair, or insecurity then you can work on freeing yourself. Imagine how much more energy you will have when the negativity is not sucking the colours of life out of everything.

The benefits of starting on a new journey of discovery will turn negative behaviours like perfectionism, self-beating, exhaustion, stubbornness, blame, living in judgement and fear into the opposite - worthiness, rest, play, trust, faith, intuition, hope, authenticity, creativity, love, belonging, joy and gratitude. How does that sound?

As we have established, the mind is very powerful and does well with repetition. It is suggested that you keep going back over these exercises until you start to notice a difference in your thinking and feeling.

Here is a quick summary of the 4 steps.

Awareness:
- Being in the moment
- Negative thoughts
- Changing perspective
- Mind gym exercises
- Setting goals
- Reflective time

Letting go:
- Acceptance
- Forgiveness
- Expectations
- Tyranny of 'should'
- Rescuing others

Reframing:
- Thinking differently
- Values
- Vision boards
- Challenging limiting beliefs

Power of language:
- Unhelpful words
- Listen to understand
- Learning from feedback
- Affirmations
- Setting your intention
- Make it happen
- Your path

What happens next?

We made it. We have arrived at a special place on **A Path Travelled** together. We are now able to reflect, to sit with the discomfort, be honest and take some new action. From here, expect to start seeing the most amazing changes. It is important to give yourself permission to be free from the old, unhelpful parts, and therefore allow yourself to see and experience other possibilities. After some patience and time, a new path will start to emerge.

Keep in mind, there will be some diversions and deviations on parts of the path, and it is from these that we learn the most. Hang in there. Keep positive thoughts and hopes clear and watch out for getting too bogged down with any confusion along the way. Aim to be open and pay close attention to the signals helping to keep you on the right path. These can so easily be missed, so keep a close eye on what unfolds and remember there will be a reason for something happening. When you are able to use the message that unfolds from each situation, this becomes like a secret weapon and is vital to your growth.

"Feeling good is the primary intention and focus..."

Dare to dream and see life differently. What will it feel like when you have arrived at a destination which allows you to be yourself? Putting attention on these positive feelings will act as a motivator for change to happen. It can be magical when there is focus in the right direction. It is not the reality changing; it's the thoughts and feelings about the reality that change. By using some, if not all these approaches, you will start to take care of YOU. There is little need to push, force or depend on willpower. Often, when we are working too hard, it is because we are working in the wrong direction.

When we are open, believe in ourselves and trust that we have the power to shape our own future, life starts to take a turn for the better. Endings are also beginnings. Pay attention to thinking and change it in areas where there is no peace. By doing so, more happiness and joy will follow, growing within you and everyone that matters.

Take some time now to think about your own Path Travelled with this book and where you are now. What are the key things you have become aware of? What have you changed? What plans do you have next?

Take some time to reflect and answer these questions:

Since the start of the book.....
- Where have I come from?
- How far have I come?
- Where am I now?
- How much further do I have to go?
- Now – what do I want and why?

Watch out for some of the magical changes once you are listening to yourself and taking the right path. You will notice wonderful feelings of contentment, joy and happiness. You will recover at a quicker rate from challenges and feel less exhausted. Positive things will come your way, you will feel healthier in mind and body and make good choices. The hard work and effort are worth it, although the journey is never easy! Remember, great sailors become great from harsher conditions rather than sailing on a millpond. This is life and we can grow from within ourselves.

I wish you all the luck in the world and remember *I believe in you.*

With love and best wishes

A SPECIAL THANKS

My life has been a path travelled and I have had the privilege and honour of sharing it with so many people. They have all pushed me, taught me, inspired me and delighted me. I dedicate this book to them all. Some of them know their impact and others don't even know how valuable they have been.

For everyone, family, friends, peers and clients who have constantly asked 'are you still writing your book?' Giving me the push and encouragement to keep going and making it happen. I feel blessed to have so many wonderful friends and people in my life and am grateful every day.

A big special thanks to my brother Paul and his family, Liz, Sam, Beth and Eve Blackler who have always been there for me. My cousin, Angela who is like a sister to me, was the first person to read the first draft, not laugh and the last before it went to the printers.

My huge gratitude to Annie Lawrenson for her patience and creativity with the typesetting and the fabulous illustrations. To Sian-Elin Flint-Freel, my first writing mentor who helped me to structure my rambling manuscript into becoming this book. To Ross Makepeace for designing the covers and Dan Dawson for my profile photograph.

I need to thank my wonderful supporters who have all helped with the reading and editing process and given valuable feedback – Jane Loughran, Tamsin Hartley, Caitlin Walker, Sue Sharp, Charlie Bennion, April Vernon and Daniel Moore.

To other friends who have successfully published books in and around the time of my writing, you spurred me on and helped me think 'I can do this' - Tamsin Hartley, Denise Chilton, Caitlin Walker and other wonderful authors I have meet and connected with at Sue Frances' Literary Lunches each year.

To Ben Corbett, my boss from Middlesbrough General Hospital who gave me the opportunity to change my career direction. Also to Steve Carter, my NLP trainer, who was one of the first people to say he believed in me and show me that I had been doing this 'stuff' all my life.

To my bestie: my dogs, Mylo and Jake, who are my company and my team! They have snored, stretched and wagged their tails every step of the way while writing this book.

About Alison Blackler

Alison is passionate about people! Watching, meeting, talking, understanding and above all supporting people to be their best.

Her personal journey has allowed her to have a job that she loves. She describes it as not really working as she loves nothing more than supporting a person, a business or a group and watching them transform. She describes every experience as teaching us something valuable and she has a desire to fast track others into this thinking.

Alison left the NHS after 25 years in 2010 and set up her own business 2minds. This has successfully supported hundreds of people to realise their potential and becoming the best version of themselves.

Alison is qualified as a Counsellor, Master Practitioner in Neuro Linguistic Programming, Clean Language Coach, practices Hypnosis and utilises all her own experiences to develop her skills.

Being a people person, Alison's family and friends are hugely important to her. She has a love of life, being outside and active and will have a go at most things! She is from the North East although now lives on the Wirral. She shares her home with her many pets.

Dear Reader

I hope you have enjoyed your journey with me.

It is my intention to have inspired you to take some steps forward in your life knowing that you can and that you have choices.

I would love to hear your thoughts, reflections and exciting life changes after reading this book.

Visit my website

www.2-minds.co.uk and sign up to my newsletter, leave a review or just have a little look round.

Visit my Facebook page

www.facebook.com/2minds

Follow me on Twitter

www.twitter.com/@alisonblackler

Connect with me on Instagram

www.instagram.com/alison2minds

I am available for public speaking and would be delighted to chat about possible events.

Wishing you all the success, happiness and love in your life........Alison.